Que® Quick Reference Series

# CorelDRAW™ Quick Reference

Mary Taylor
James Karney

Que® Corporation
Carmel, Indiana

*CorelDraw Quick Reference.*

Copyright ©1990 by Que Corporation.

Library of Congress Catalog Number: 90-62077

ISBN 0-88022-597-1

93   92   91   90                4   3   2   1

Interpretation of the printing code: the rightmost double-digit number is the year of the book's printing; the rightmost single-digit number is the number of the book's printing. For example, a printing code of 90-4 shows that the fourth printing of the book occurred in 1990.

**Publishing Director**
Lloyd J. Short

**Series Product Director**
Karen A. Bluestein

**Senior Production Editor**
Cheryl S. Robinson

**Technical Editor**
James Karney

**Proofreaders**
Charles A. Hutchinson
Betty Kish

**Indexer**
Jill Bomaster

**Editorial Assistant**
Patricia J. Brooks

**Production**
Brad Chinn
Denny Hager

# Que Quick Reference Series

The *Que Quick Reference Series* is a portable resource of essential microcomputer knowledge. Whether you are a new or experienced user, you can rely on the high-quality information contained in these convenient guides.

Drawing on the experience of many of Que's best-selling authors, the *Que Quick Reference Series* helps you easily access important program information.

Now it's easy to look up often-used commands and functions for programs such as 1-2-3, dBASE IV, WordPerfect 5, Microsoft Word 5, and MS-DOS, as well as programming information for C, Turbo Pascal, and QuickBASIC 4.

Use the *Que Quick Reference Series* as a compact alternative to confusing and complicated traditional documentation.

The *Que Quick Reference Series* includes these titles:

*1-2-3 Quick Reference*
*1-2-3 Release 2.2 Quick Reference*
*1-2-3 Release 3 Quick Reference*
*Allways Quick Reference*
*Assembly Language Quick Reference*
*AutoCAD Quick Reference*
*C Quick Reference*
*dBASE IV Quick Reference*
*DOS and BIOS Functions Quick Reference*
*Excel Quick Reference*
*Hard Disk Quick Reference*
*Harvard Graphics Quick Reference*
*MS-DOS Quick Reference*
*Microsoft Word 5 Quick Reference*

*Norton Utilities Quick Reference*
*PC Tools Quick Reference*
*Q&A Quick Reference*
*QuickBASIC Quick Reference*
*Turbo Pascal Quick Reference*
*UNIX Programmer's Quick Reference*
*WordPerfect Quick Reference*
*UNIX Shell Commands Quick Reference*
*Windows 3 Quick Reference*
*WordPerfect 5.1 Quick Reference*

## *Trademark Acknowledgments*

1-2-3 and Lotus are registered trademarks of Lotus Development Corporation.Adobe Systems Incorporated.

Apple LaserWriter is a registered trademark of Apple Computer, Inc.

Bitstream is a registered trademark of Bitstream Inc.

CoreDRAW! is a registered trademark of Corel Systems Corporation.

dBASE, dBASE III Plus, and dBASE IV are registered trademarks of Ashton-Tate Corporation.

Epson FX-80 is a trademark, and EPSON is a registered trademark of Epson Corporation.

Hercules Graphics Card is a trademark of Hercules Computer Technology.

HP DeskJet, LaserJet, and DeskJet Plus are trademarks of Hewlett-Packard Co.

IBM, IBM PC, and IBM AT are registered trademarks, and IBM PC XT is a trademark of International Business Machines Corporation.

LaserWriter and Macintosh are registered trademarks of Apple Computer Inc.

Microsoft Windows and Microsoft Word are registered trademarks of Microsoft Corporation.

PageMaker is a registered trademark of Aldus Corporation.

PANTONE is a registered trademark of Pantone Inc.

PostScript is a registered trademark of Adobe Systems Incorporated.

Publisher's Type Foundry is a trademark of ZSoft Corporation.

Ventura Publisher is registered trademark of Ventura Software, Inc.

# Table of Contents

# Introduction

*CorelDraw Quick Reference* is not a rehash of traditional documentation. Instead, this quick reference is a compilation of the most frequently used functions and commands from Corel System's CorelDraw program.

*CorelDraw Quick Reference* presents essential information on CorelDraw commands and functions. You learn the proper use of primary CorelDraw functions, as well as how to navigate through the program's system of menus. This book contains fundamental information in a compact, easy-to-use format.

*CorelDraw Quick Reference* is divided into sections. The first section, CorelDraw Basics, contains the basic information you need to understand how you can use this program to suit you. The Command Reference is an alphabetical listing of all CorelDraw commands. Each command is presented in the same format. A brief introductory paragraph provides an explanation of each command. The Procedures sections provide step-by-step instructions. Periodically throughout the book, you will find Tips and Notes. These sections help you use CorelDraw's features successfully. The last section of the book is devoted to CorelTrace.

Now you can put essential information at your fingertips with Allways Quick Reference—and the entire Que Quick Reference Series!

# HINTS FOR USING THIS BOOK

*CorelDraw Quick Reference* is a task-oriented book that enables you easily to look up any topic on which you need information. Just turn to the alphabetical command listing in the Table of Contents, or use the more comprehensive index.

As you read this book, keep the following conventions in mind:

- All keys you press and information you type appear in boldfaced **blue** type.

- All messages that appear on-screen are shown in a `digital` typeface.

- All menu names, options, and icons that you select with the mouse appear in boldfaced **blue** type.

This book contains three major sections. The first section introduces CorelDraw and provides some basic information. The Command Reference contains an alphabetical command listing with step-by-step procedures. The third section explains CorelTrace.

## CorelDraw Basics

CorelDraw is an impressive software package that has won virtually every major industry award for excellence. With this program, you can create business drawings, commercial illustrations, and color or black and white art for publications.

Draw programs create illustrations in vector format, which means that the object is described mathematically as a series of curves and lines. CorelDraw also can treat any object (including text) as a bezier curve (pronounced bez-e-ay) curve. Bezier curves are special because they have handles that enable you to shape them.

With CorelDraw, you also can import images from a paint program, or images that were captured with a scanner. The image can be tinted, rotated, and included as part of a drawing, or portions can be traced into vector elements and the original removed.

The program's capability to accept input from a wide variety of file formats also lets you incorporate clip art from many sources and even use artwork designed on a Macintosh. Because the file conversion feature works both ways, CorelDraw can export in both vector and bitmap file formats. This capability lets you use drawings from CorelDraw on almost any computer, including IBM mainframes and the Apple Macintosh.

CorelDraw comes with 102 high quality fonts. The program can convert fonts by vendors such as Bitstream and Adobe, or fonts created with programs such as ZSoft's Publisher's Type Foundry, into a form it can use with the free utility WFMBOSS that is included with your program disks.

The capability to produce complex radial, linear, and Postscript fills, combined with full PANTONE, process, and spot color support, gives CorelDraw users a host of techniques for designing attention-getting artwork.

Packaged with the program disks are a number of example drawings. A companion set of clip art files (ready to use items such as computers and road signs) can be imported into your illustrations. Provided by a variety of vendors, these collections help you achieve professional results.

The images produced with CorelDraw can be exported to a typesetter, printed on a high quality color printer, or converted into beautiful slides. Service bureaus are available so that anyone can achieve top notch output.

If you have not used draw-type programs, copy the example files to your hard disk so that you can see how they were made. You will find many useful hints in these files. The clip art file, however, is quite large and takes up too much hard disk space. Do not copy these files to your hard disk. Keep the disks and the accompanying catalog handy. Then you can copy any specific file as the need arises.

Although CorelDraw supports any printer that has a Microsoft Windows driver, not all printers are created equal. Some of the more complex fills and other

features only print on a Postscript printer. The early
Apple LaserWriters may not print some complicated
drawings.

## Installation

To use CorelDraw, you must have at least an AT-class
personal computer (80286). More advanced computers,
such as the 80386 and 80486, offer faster operation.
The program does not run on the original IBM PC or
other 8080-based computers. Any system configuration
that can run Windows 286, Windows 386, or Windows
3.0 can run CorelDraw. To take full advantage of
CorelDraw, a VGA color monitor and card are
recommended, and you must have a mouse or other
pointing device that is compatible with Windows.

Installing CorelDraw and CorelTrace is very simple.
You must have a full version of Microsoft Windows
2.0 or later on the system. Make sure that you know
the name of the directory in which Windows is located.
Insert the CorelDraw program disk, change the DOS
prompt to that drive, and type INSTALL. Follow the
instructions to change disks. Note that CorelDraw
cannot be installed by just copying the disks. The
installation routine modifies the Windows WIN.INI
file, and the programs are in a condensed form that has
to be expanded.

## Using the Mouse

CorelDraw requires that you use a mouse or graphics
tablet. You can use any Microsoft-compatible mouse.
To select objects with the mouse, click the left button.
This process is referred to as *clicking*.

In Corel Draw, some of the actions, such as rotating an
object, require that you *double-click* on an object. To
double-click the mouse, rapidly press the left button
twice.

Moving and resizing objects in Corel Draw is a simple
*drag* procedure. Dragging is done by pressing and
holding the left button as you move the mouse. If you
want to change the mouse sensitivity for clicking and

double-clicking, refer to the Microsoft Windows Users Guide. The response can be modified with the Windows Control Panel.

## *The Desktop Environment*

CorelDraw takes full advantage of the Windows' user interface. The following figure shows the Windows Desktop Controls. The numbers correspond to the definitions list below the figure.

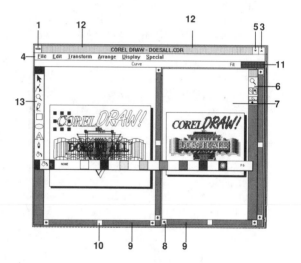

| **1** Control menu | Offers the options Restore, Move, Size, Minimize, Maximize, Close, and Switch To. |
| --- | --- |
| **2** Icon | Displays a small picture if an application is minimized or yet to be activated. |
| **3** Maximize button | Expands the open window. |
| **4** Menu bar | Displays the menu items used to control the application. |

| | |
|---|---|
| **5** Minimize button | Reduces the size of the window. |
| **6** Preview Toolbox | Provides a set of icons that control the Preview window display. |
| **7** Preview window | Displays the drawing as it will appear after printing. (Some features do not appear, such as Postscript textures.) |
| **8** Scroll Arrow | Controls the scroll box. |
| **9** Scroll bar | Combines the action of the scroll arrows and scroll box. |
| **10** Scroll Box | Displays your file position. Can be dragged to move your position in the file. |
| **11** Status Line | Provides information on selected object, current operation, and fills. |
| **12** Title bar | Tells you the name of the program and data file if applicable, or the name of the dialog box. |
| **13** Toolbox | Provides nine tools that enable you to draw and select objects. |
| **14** Window | The entire entity made up of at least a Control menu, Title bar, and borders. |
| **15** Window border | The outside frame of the window. |

Windows applications, such as CorelDraw, often use dialog boxes to enable you to make a group of related choices. The following figure shows a CorelDraw dialog box:

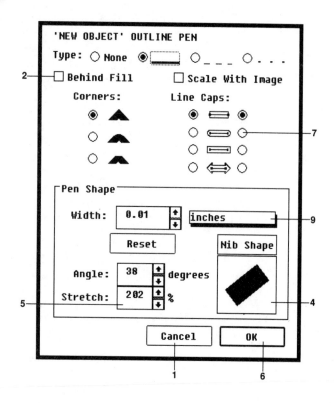

| 1 Cancel button | Closes a dialog box. Ignores any changes made. |
| 2 Checkbox | Indicates (with an "x") when a selection has been made. |
| 3 Command button | Opens another dialog box or directly executes a command. Cancel and OK buttons are examples of command buttons. |
| 4 Display box | Shows a sample of a current selection. |
| 5 Numeric entry box | Sets a value for an option, such as point size or degree of enlargement. |

**6** OK button     Confirms that you are finished with the dialog box and want to execute your choices.

**7** Radio button     Circles that toggle on and off. When the selection is made, the center of the button will be black.

**8** Scroll arrow     Changes values up or down when holding your left mouse button causes the values to keep changing.

**9** Variable unit box     Enables you to change the unit of measure.

# Corel Interface

Unlike complicated CAD (Computer Aided Design Programs) that take months to learn, CorelDraw has only a few tools that you must master. CorelDraw uses a combination of pull-down menus and nine tools to create and arrange elements on the page. Work is done in a *wireframe* mode, which means you see the outline of objects in a window and can see a full view in another preview window. This process improves the speed of the program and gives you flexibility in handling the screen display to suit the task at hand.

Each object you create consists of two parts: an outer border called the outline, and the inner area known as the fill. Each part can be controlled independently of the other.

Objects used in CorelDraw illustrations can be broken down into the following basic groups:

- bitmaps (which are imported)
- freehand shapes
- text
- lines and curves
- circles and ellipses
- rectangles and squares

Unlike paint programs that use a collection of dots to create artwork and produce a bitmap image, CorelDraw combines these elements and arranges the parts in layers to create the finished drawing.

You can set the Corel screen to show the entire working area or the portion that will be printed. You also can magnify any part of the drawing to fill the window. Scroll bars let you shift the viewing area, and a Preview window shows exactly what the printed result will be.

The CorelDraw tools are arranged in a column on the left side of the screen and enable you to draw and manipulate objects, insert text, change the magnification, and work this the shape, fill and color of the design.

# Corel Menus

Menus offer access to file services and commands that enhance or modify the tools. The menus also enable you to customize how CorelDraw works to suit you. You can control the action of a command, and even record a series of commands.

The pull-down menus provide access to services such as importing images, printing, combining groups of objects, and setting options on how the program operates. In addition, you can use the menus to perform some of the same functions as the tools and to create or use macros.

As you open menus, note that some of the items are in a shade of gray and others are black. The gray tone indicates that the option is not available.

The more complicated commands and options may require that you work with a supplemental dialog box. A brief explanation of the purpose of each menu follows. For more detailed information on using a specific function, refer to the appropriate listing in the Command Reference.

### The File Menu

The File menu contains the commands that deal with opening and closing files and printing and saving your work.

The New option opens a new file and gives you a blank page. Make sure that you save any work you want to keep before using this command. The Open command enables you to reopen an existing CorelDraw (CDR) file.

The Save command writes the current drawing to disk. The Save As option enables you to assign a different name than the one used to open an existing file. You will find this feature handy when you want to create two versions of a drawing.

The File Menu also provides access to files created in other programs, and even permits you to bring in scanned images saved in the PC Paintbrush (PCX) or Tagged Image File format (TIF). If you want to use a Corel drawing in Ventura Publisher, PageMaker, or some other program, the Export option provides a way to convert the CorelDraw file into a format that can be used by many other applications. This menu also controls access to the printer, page setup controls, and the Quit function.

### The Edit Menu

This menu provides shortcuts and help when you make a mistake. The Undo and Redo commands permit you to undo the last action you performed and to return the settings to the way they were before the last command was issued.

You can use this menu to cut, copy, paste, clear, or duplicate any object or group of objects. You can modify text that is already on the page and copy attributes from one block to another.

### The Transform Menu

Although this menu contains only three commands, it offers some of the most powerful tools for changing the appearance of an object.

You can rotate a chosen object, while twisting and turning it almost inside out. Leaving an original copy as you make a duplicate in another position is a quick and easy method for designing shadow and pinwheel effects.

The Clear Transformation option lets you remove any changes you make to a design element.

## The Arrange Menu

This collection of commands provides a way to order the freeform environment of a CorelDraw illustration. You can arrange the relative order of objects. You can combine or group several objects to change attributes, such as color or fill with one command. You also can break groups apart after the transformation is completed.

Use this menu to precisely align objects on each other. This feature is very handy, for example, in centering items on the page.

One very powerful command in this menu is Fit Text To Path. You can make a line of text take on virtually any shape you want.

## The Display Menu

With the options available in the Display menu, you can force objects to line up on an invisible grid, display rulers for measuring spacing, and control operation of the Preview window.

## The Special Menu

CorelDraw includes this menu for two purposes. You can record and reuse a series of commands. Macros can be defined and saved to disk so that you don't have to repeat a series of keystrokes manually.

You also can customize some of the program defaults. The Preferences option controls such things as how close together two lines can be drawn before they will be joined together. You also can set things such as which letter will be shown in the Typeface Section Box and how the Auto-Trace command works.

# CorelDraw Tools

To use this Quick Reference and successfully operate CorelDraw, you must understand the Toolbox. The Toolbox contains nine tools that are arranged on the left side of the screen. Many of the tools have more than one use. Some of the tools open flyout menus, providing several options for their use. Many of the menu functions can be duplicated by using the appropriate tool. Together these tools offer a complete art supply store in an electronic form.

The Toolbox can be divided into three groups: drawing, editing, and attribute tools. The drawing tools create objects such as circles, text, and lines. Editing tools modify the shape and form of exiting elements of an illustration. The attribute tools control the type of outline and fill that the parts of the drawing have.

The Control and Shift keys have an effect on certain toolbox operations. These keys are mentioned as appropriate in the Command Reference. Corel refers to the Control key as the Constrain tool. For more information on this feature see *Constrain*.

You may want to experiment with each of the tools and the mouse before using the Command Reference. Very little practice is required to make their use second nature.

The following sections briefly explain the tools in the order they appear on the Corel screen. For a more complete explanation of the specific operations, refer to the appropriate topic in the command reference.

## *The Pick Tool*

Although the Pick tool does not place objects on the screen, it is one of the most often used tools. After you select the Pick tool and click once on an object, you can shape the object by dragging the nodes and perform many of the Menu Bar transformations.

Double-clicking on an object causes a series of arrows to appear within the highlight box. You can use these handles literally to pull the object inside out.

You can select all objects by dragging the Pick tool from a point outside a group of objects to another point diagonally beyond the objects. You then can perform actions as if the various elements were one. Unselect an object or group of objects by clicking the mouse once on a blank portion of the screen.

When the Pick tool is selected, the Status Line shows the type of object selected, such as line, rectangle, or bitmap, or the number of objects in a group.

You can activate the Pick tool by pressing the space bar once. Pressing the space bar again reactivates the tool you were working with last.

### *The Shape Tool*

The Shape tool alters the shape of a curve. You can convert lines to curves, change a curve to a line, and add new or delete existing segments. Use the Shape tool to edit all bezier elements so that you can match or create a desired form. The Shape tool cursor appears as a wedge. This tool is used on text to change the interline spacing, kerning, and baseline relationships.

### *The Zoom Tool*

The third tool in the CorelDraw Toolbox looks like a magnifying glass. Selecting this tool opens a flyout menu. CorelDraw flyout menus open as a strip with several icons offering different options for that tool. In this case, you can select one of several preset magnifications, or use the magnifying glass with the plus symbol to select any portion of the drawing to fill the working area. After you use the Zoom tool, Corel automatically returns action to the previously selected tool.

### *The Freehand Tool*

The Freehand tool looks like a pencil with the sharpened end pointing to the lower left. With this tool, you can draw objects in the working area. (Corel permits you to draw elements outside the box that defines the printed page.)

You can use the Freehand Tool to create a straight line
or to draw a freehand shape or curve. You also can
combine the two types of drawings to create polygons
with both straight and freehand sections. Another use
of the Freehand tool involves tracing portions of an
image.

### The Rectangle Tool

This tool enables you to create both rectangles and
squares. The cursor for this tool resembles a thin set of
crosshairs.

To use the tool, place the cursor at the starting point
and drag the mouse at an angle. The object is placed
when you release the left mouse button.

### The Ellipse Tool

This tool is similar to the Rectangle tool, except it is
used to draw circles and ellipses. The cursor is the
same crosshair shape, and you draw ellipses by
dragging the mouse at an angle from the starting point
until the object looks the way you want. Using the
Constrain key with the Ellipse tool results in a perfect
circular form.

### The Text Tool

The A-shaped object in the Toolbox is the Text tool.
You use this tool to enter text, and set many of the
typographical attributes. The Text tool cursor
resembles an I-beam shape.

Adding text to an illustration may seem a little strange
to those not used to draw software. CorelDraw is not a
word processor. The text is really a special type of
object. The cursor is placed where the text is to appear,
and the mouse button pressed once. This action
generates a dialog box over the working area of the
screen. The area at the top of the box is the text entry
area. The cursor in the rectangle lets you type up to
250 characters.

The selection box in the lower left part of the dialog
box lets you choose the font to be displayed. The large

letter (usually a capital A) in the lower right portion of the dialog box is a sample of the currently selected font. Point sizes can be set as desired in the box above the sample character, but spacing must be set in another box. Font attributes such as bold and italic vary with the exact typeface chosen.

### The Outline Tool

The Outline tool looks like the nib on a fountain pen. With this tool, you control the width, color, and shape of the outline of an object. When you select the Outline tool, a flyout menu is displayed.

The upper set of options on the flyout bar sets the pen shape, angle, and the type of line drawn. Clicking again on the pen shape at the left of the flyout menu opens a dialog box that offers a range of customizing features. Some features require a Postscript printer. The lower half of the bar is used to select the color or shade of the outline area.

Click on the brush icon in the left-hand corner to see a dialog box. This dialog box provides complete control over the color of the outline area.

The use of this tool has nothing to do with the way the wireframe will appear in the working window, only in the Preview Window and in the final output. For more information on the options for this tool, see *Outline Attributes* in the Command Reference.

### The Fill Tool

Each object in a drawing has two parts—an outline and a fill. The paint bucket icon at the bottom of the Toolbox opens a flyout menu. You can use this menu and its dialog box (obtained by clicking on the left-most icon of the flyout bar) to control the shade, color,

and pattern of the fill area. Clicking on the word NONE
on the bar removes the fill from the object. Other
shades are white, black, and shades ranging from 10 to
80 percent gray. The last two blocks open the dialog
boxes for radial/linear fills and Postscript textures.

# COMMAND REFERENCE

## About

### Purpose

Tells you the date and version number of the
CorelDraw program that is used on the system. This
information helps you know which features are
available, and aids Corel's technical support team
when you call for assistance.

### To obtain the date and version number of CorelDraw

1. Click on and open the **Windows Control** menu
   (the box that looks like a minus symbol in the
   upper-left corner of the window) with any tool.

2. Select **About**.

   The Corel copyright information and program
   version number appear in a box. Note both the
   date and number.

### Note

If you want to know more about the program, consult
the last section in the Technical Reference Guide. This
section provides a history of CorelDraw development
and enhancements.

# Align Text To Baseline

### Purpose

Resets the vertical shift to zero in relation to the original baseline. This command does not reverse the effect of any rotation. Rotated characters are aligned relative to the angle of rotation.

### To reset the vertical shift

1. Select the **Pick** tool from the Toolbox.

2. Select the text object.

3. From the **Arrange** menu, select **Align To Baseline**.

### Keyboard Shortcut

**Alt-A-L**

# Alignment

### Purpose

Aligns the currently selected objects vertically and horizontally in relation to each other on the page.

### To align objects

1. Select the **Pick** tool from the Toolbox.

2. Select the objects you want aligned with the Shift-click method or the Marquee Selection box method.

3. From the **Align** menu, select **Align**.

   The Align dialog box appears.

4. Select the **Vertical** or **Horizontal** options. You can select both options at once.

5. Click **OK** to confirm your choices or **Cancel** to abandon the operation.

*Note*

The object that is the farthest from the chosen direction remains in the same place, but all other objects move. If the center is selected, all objects may shift. Selecting Center in both Horizontal and Vertical positions may hide smaller objects under larger objects.

# Arcs and Wedges

*Purpose*

Enables you to use the Shape tool to create arcs from any object drawn with the Ellipse tool. The arc is a basic shape used in many drawings and is really a portion of a circle or ellipse. The arc can be combined with other lines and curves to produce polygon shapes.

*To create an arc*

1. Select the Shape tool from the Toolbox.

2. Select the circle or ellipse you want to modify.

3. Place the point of the Shape tool on the node located at the top or bottom of the object.

4. Drag the mouse around the outside of the object (drawing inside the object creates a pie wedge).

5. Release the mouse button after you achieve the desired result.

*To create a pie shape or wedge*

1. Select the Shape tool from the Toolbox.

2. Select the circle or ellipse you want to modify.

3. Place the point of the Shape tool on the node located at the top or bottom of the object.

4. Drag the mouse around the inside of the object (drawing outside the object creates an arc).

5. Release the mouse button after you achieve the desired result.

*Tip*

If you need to draw an arc or pie shape in a multiple of 15 degrees (15, 30, or 45), press and hold the Control key as you draw the arc. This procedure limits the changes to 15 degree increments.

*Notes*

The Status Line shows the word Ellipse, the angles involved (such as 66.6 to 270.0 degrees), and the total angle. If the word Distorted appears after the total angle, the object is not cut from a perfect circle.

The handles on the highlighting box appear as if the entire ellipse had been drawn. Seeing the whole shape aids in creating things such as exploded views.

# Auto-Update

*Purpose*

Turns on and off the automatic operation of the Preview window. If Auto-Update is selected, the Preview screen shows all changes as they are made to the drawing. With the option disabled, you must click on the Preview window area to update the information. Because the working area only shows a wireframe of your objects, you must use Preview to see how lines and fills will appear in the finished product.

*To activate Auto-Update*

1. If the Preview window is not visible, use any tool to open the Display menu and select Show Preview.

The screen splits in half and the drawing, including any shading, appears in the Preview screen to the right of the Draw screen.

2. From the Display menu, select **Auto-Update**

An arrow appears to the left of the selection.

To turn off Auto-Update, simply select **Auto-Update** from the **Display** menu a second time.

### Keyboard Shortcut

**Alt-D-A**

### Notes

If you use the scroll bars to change the visible working area, the Preview window does not change until the drawing is modified, even if Auto-Update is selected.

Turning off this feature speeds up your work because the computer does not have to redraw the Preview window.

# Backups

### Purpose

Creates a backup copy of your work under another name when you save modifications to a CorelDraw file. This feature is handy when you decide to use a previous version. You must modify the WIN.INI file that Windows uses to set defaults.

### To set up CorelDraw to make backup files

1. Run any editor or word processor that works with and writes an ASCII (plain) text file. (Windows 3 users can use the SysEdit utility that comes with Windows.)

2. Make a backup copy of the WIN.INI file under the name **WIN.OLD**. (You can rename this file if you decide not to keep a backup, or if you make a mistake in editing.)

3. Load the WIN.INI file in the text editor (not the WIN.OLD you just made).

4. Find the section of the file that has the heading
   `[CDrawConfig]`.

5. Edit the line that reads `MakebackupWhenSave`
   to read **MakeBackupWhenSave=1.**

6. Save the file as WIN.INI in the directory that
   contains the Windows program files (usually
   \Windows).

7. Exit Windows and start Windows again.

   Each time you save a CorelDraw file with the
   .CDR extension, the old file (the last version
   saved) will be renamed with a .BAK extension.

*Notes*

If you need the older version or a drawing, it can be
renamed and used like any other .CDR drawing.

To turn off the backup feature, simply rename
WIN.OLD to WIN.INI.

# ═ Break Apart

*Purpose*

Permits you to change a multi-segment curve or
several objects joined with the Combine command into
a collection of single segments. This command is the
opposite of the Combine command. Use this command
to correct overlapping lines in a complex object, or use
different fills and outline strokes in a complex object
or string of text that has been converted to curves.

*To change a multi-segment curve into a collection of single
segments*

1. Select the **Pick** tool.

2. Select the multi-segment object.

3. From the **Arrange** Menu, select **Break Apart**

   The group is now a collection of individual
   segments and can be manipulated as such.

*Keyboard Shortcut*

Press **Alt-A-B** after you select the object with the **Pick** tool.

*Notes*

If you want to break apart a block of text that is not part of a combined object, you first must convert the text to curves.

You cannot break apart bitmapped or grouped objects.

Be careful when you use this command. The combined object may contain text you do not want converted to curves. The command automatically converts each separate closed path (such as an O) into an individual curve. After the conversion, you cannot treat it as a text object, and it may result in some unwanted filled sections.

# Calligraphic Effects

*Purpose*

Creates outlines that look as if they had been drawn with a calligraphic pen. Adjustments let you modify the width, shape, and angle of the pen to customize the effect. You can use this feature with lines, curves, and text elements.

*To obtain calligraphic effects*

1. Select the **Pick** tool.

2. Select the object you want outlined.

3. Open the **Outline** menu (the pen nib in the Toolbox).

4. Select the **Pen** shape from the flyout menu.

   The Outline Pen dialog box appears. Use the Pen Shape section to choose from the following options:

- Set the width in the box by typing a number on your keyboard or using the arrows.

- Adjust the nib angle by typing or using the arrows.

- Adjust the stretch option by typing or using the arrows.

5. Click **OK** to confirm the operation.

*Notes*

Note that if you do not perform Steps 1 and 2, the values you enter become the new Pen Shape defaults.

To reset the Pen to the zero angle and 100 percent stretch defaults, click on the Reset button.

The Nib Shape box shows how the Pen Nib will look at the current settings.

You can change the unit of measure by clicking on the current value next to the Width Entry box. Options include Inches, Picas and Points, Fractional Points, or Centimeters.

A line set to a width of 0.00 produces the smallest line that the output device can produce. If you are working with a 300 lines per inch (lpi) laser, the line will be one pixel tall, or 1/300th of an inch. If you print the same file on a typesetter at 2500 lpi, it will take a very good eye to see the line. By the same token, a 72 lpi dot-matrix printer will output a one point thick line. If you want no line at all, use the None option.

# Character Attributes

*Purpose*

Changes the appearance of individual letters or a complete block of text in an illustration. Among the things you can redefine are typeface, style, size, horizontal and vertical shifts, and angle. You cannot perform a character edit with Character Attributes.

### *To change attributes for a portion of the text string*

1. Select the Shape tool from the Toolbox.

2. Use one of the following methods to select the characters you want to modify:

   • Double-click on the node to the left of the character.

   • Click on more than one character's node as you press and hold Shift. Then double-click on another node.

   • Draw a Marquee Selection box around the nodes with the Shape tool, and double-click on one of the nodes.

   The nodes of the selected characters change to black as they are selected.

   The Character Attributes dialog box appears.

3. Make the desired changes and click OK.

   The dialog box disappears and the text objects are modified.

### *Notes*

You can modify selected characters using the following attribute options that are provided in the Character Attribute dialog box:

| | |
|---|---|
| Typeface | Selects typeface. Click on the up- and down-arrows to scroll through the list of choices and click on the typeface name you want. The active selection appears highlighted. |
| Point Size | Selects point size. Enter the desired size or click on the up- and down-arrow keys to change the point size. The position of other characters changes (even unselected ones) if the size is changed too much. |

**Style**

Selects Normal, Bold, Italic, and Bold Italic. Change the style of the chosen typeface by clicking the circle that appears next to the style name. If a radio button is gray, that option is not available.

**Horizontal Shift**

Moves individual characters closer together or farther apart. You can enter the exact value of the shift or click on the **up-** and **down-arrow** keys.

The unit of measure for this setting is an *em*. The exact size of an em varies and is equal to the width of an uppercase M in the same typeface and font. Using ems results in a balanced appearance based on the size of type used.

**Vertical Shift**

Moves characters up and down relative to the baseline. You can enter the exact value of the shift or click on the **up-** and **down-arrows**.

Vertical Shift is measured in a percent of the point size used for the entire text string, not for the one set in this Character Attribute box.

**Character Angle**

Rotates characters in relation to the baseline. A positive angle shifts the character in a clockwise rotation; negative values shift the character counterclockwise in relation to the baseline. Using this option may change the position of other characters in the string.

## Tips

Make any changes to text with this option before you use the Convert Text To Curves command. After text is converted, you cannot edit the text or modify character attributes.

If you do not want the character spacing to change, use Edit Text and set the alignment to none (instead of left, center, or right) before using the Character Attributes command.

# Circles and Ellipses

## Purpose

Draws perfect circles and ellipses with the Ellipse tool. You can use several options to control the way the object is created and placed on the page.

## To create an ellipse

1. Select the **Ellipse** tool from the Toolbox.

   The cursor changes to a hairline cross, and the Ellipse tool is highlighted.

2. Place the cursor where you want the upper left of the ellipse to begin.

3. Drag the mouse in the desired direction.

4. Release the mouse button when you are satisfied with the ellipse shape.

## To create a circle

1. Select the **Ellipse** tool from the Toolbox.

   The cursor changes to a hairline cross, and the Ellipse tool is highlighted.

2. Place the cursor where you want the upper left of the circle to begin.

3. Press and hold the **Control** key.

4. Drag the mouse in the desired direction.

5. Release the mouse button when you are satisfied with the circle.

6. Release the Control key.

   If you release the Control key before you release the mouse button, you may not get a perfect circle.

*Note*

The Status Line shows the dimensions of the object as you drag the mouse. After you release the mouse button, displays the word Ellipse.

# Clear

*Purpose*

Removes an object or objects from the drawing. The deleted material is not placed in the Clipboard.

*To remove an object*

1. Select the Pick or Shape tool from the Toolbox.

2. Click on the object you want removed. To select multiple objects, press and hold the Shift key as you click the mouse or draw a Marquee Selection box around the object.

3. Press Del.

   or

   From the Edit menu, select Clear.

   The selected objects are removed from the screen.

*Note*

If you Clear an object by mistake, use the Undo function immediately. If you use any other command, the cleared object cannot be recovered.

# Clear Transformations

### Purpose

Resets all rotating, skewing, sizing, and scaling operations on an object. After the command is applied, the object is returned to the appearance it had when it was first drawn.

### To reset all size and placement operations

1. Select the Pick Tool.

2. Click on the object or draw a Marquee Selection box around a group of objects.

3. From the Transform menu, select Clear Transformations.

### Keyboard Shortcut

Alt-T-C

### Notes

Rotation and skew settings are returned to zero degrees and the center of gravity (bullseye) is centered.

Sizing and scaling are set to 100 percent, and text is returned to the point size chosen when it was created.

When applied to a group of objects, this command removes all transformations from the selected group and all transformations made to any individual components of a group.

# Clip Art

### Purpose

Consists of electronic images that you can import into CorelDraw. Designers and illustrators often take advantage of ready-to-use drawings to create layouts. In the past, these drawings were purchased in book form from vendors. With your CorelDraw package came several disks that contain clip art samples and a catalog showing what is available. Clip art can add a professional touch to newsletters and flyers.

### To import clip art

1. Identify the file name, file format, and path location of the clip art you want to import.

   An example is NEATPIC.PCX on drive A.

2. Use any tool to open the **File** menu.

3. Select **Import**.

4. Choose the proper file type for the clip art you want to import to your drawing.

5. Click **OK**.

   The File Selection box appears.

6. Change to the proper drive and directory if required.

7. Double-click on file name, or single-click on the name and then click **Open**.

   The file appears in your drawing when the dialog box disappears.

### Keyboard Shortcut

Press **Alt-F-I,** select the file format, and double-click on the file name.

### Tips

Do not keep clip art files on your hard disk unless you use them regularly. Clip art tends to require a lot of space and is just as easily stored on floppy disks.

The sample clip art supplied with CorelDraw contains more than 340 drawings in a variety of file formats. The catalog shows each piece of art and lists the file type and clip art disk. Not only is this the best way to locate these files, but it enables you to see which file formats work best with your style and printer.

### Notes

If the format you selected does not work, make sure that you chose the format that matches your file. If the format is correct, problems may be due to variations in the format standard.

You can use any of the available file format types listed in the Import menu as sources for clip art. Availability of clip art varies, depending on the version of CorelDraw you have. The newer releases have more options.

Although the files provided with the CorelDraw program all work well, there are limitations in what can be imported into the program for various formats. Clip art created with other programs may not behave as expected. Always test first to avoid disappointment. See *Import* and the Technical Reference Supplement that was provided by CorelDraw for more information.

# Close Path

### *Purpose*

Joins the two ends of an open path so that you may fill or shade the object.

### *To close an open path*

1. Select the Shape tool.

2. Locate the end nodes that you want to join.

3. Draw a Marquee Selection box around both nodes or Shift-Click.

4. Double-click on either node.

   The Node Edit menu appears.

5. Select Join.

   You now can shade or fill the closed object.

### *Tip*

Use the Zoom tool to enlarge the area before you select the nodes.

# Combine

## *Purpose*

Enables you to join several objects into a single curved object. These objects do not have to be physically connected. Non-curved objects automatically convert to curved objects when you execute the command. By combining objects, you can use the Shape tool on many nodes at once to smooth an object's appearance, or join two lines or curves into a single element.

The Combine tool cannot be used to join objects with different attributes, such as bitmaps and ellipses.

Combining objects may improve redrawing time and memory availability. You also can create masks so that you can view an underlying object.

## *To combine objects*

1. Select the **Pick** tool from the Toolbox.

2. Press and hold the **Shift** key as you click on the objects you want combined.

   or

   Draw a Marquee Selection box around the objects.

3. From the **Arrange** menu, select **Combine**.

   The objects are now combined, even if they do not touch.

## *Notes*

Corel creates a new object for each line or curve drawn with the Freehand tool. Complex drawings that contain over 1,000 objects may result in noticeably slower performance. The Combine option reduces the memory requirements, improves program performance, and may speed printing.

If you use Combine on objects that include text elements, the text is converted to curves and cannot be changed back. Therefore, always finish all text editing before you use Combine.

# Constrain

## *Purpose*

Enables you to do such things as create perfect circles and squares and to draw lines at precisely set angles. The simple nine member Toolbox makes CorelDraw easy to use, but it also means that the software designers had to find ways to let users accurately draw objects with fewer tools than other high-end draw programs.

## *To use Constrain in the various operations*

1. Select the appropriate CorelDraw tool.

2. Press and hold the **Constrain** (Control) key, and then release the mouse button.

The following list shows the Constrain combinations. Each tool that applies is listed in its Toolbox order of appearance, along with the Constrain controls available.

### Pick Tool

| | |
|---|---|
| Stretch and scale | Limits the changes to 100 percent increments (100%, 200%, etc.). Dragging the mouse results in a perfect mirror image. |
| While moving an object | Limits the action to the vertical and horizontal axis. You cannot move an object diagonally with the Constrain key depressed. |
| Rotating and skewing | Limits the motion to 15 degree increments and shifts the center of rotation to the center point to one of the eight delimiters on the highlighting box. |

## Shape Tool

| | |
|---|---|
| Drawing arcs and wedges | Causes the angle to be created in 15 degree increments. |
| Moving control points and nodes | Limits the action to the vertical and horizontal axis. You cannot move a control point or node diagonally while holding the Constrain key. |

## Freehand Tool

| | |
|---|---|
| Drawing straight lines | Draws the line exactly on the vertical or horizontal, or at an angle which is a multiple of 15 degrees. |

## Rectangle Tool

| | |
|---|---|
| Drawing a square | Results in a perfectly square object. |

## Ellipse Tool

| | |
|---|---|
| Drawing a circle | Results in a perfectly circular object. |

# ControlPoints

### *Purpose*

Enables you to control the shape of a curve as it passes through a node. By pulling and moving the control points, the size and shape of adjacent segments of a curve can be precisely manipulated. You see the results as changes are made.

### *To control the shape of a curve*

1. Select the Shape tool from the Toolbox.

2. Click on the desired node.

The control points become visible.

3. Adjust the position of the node or control point by placing the **Shape** tool over the handle and dragging.

Moving a node shortens or lengthens the curve and can alter the shape of the line.

You can drag the control point handle to change the way the curve passes through the node. Doing so increases or decreases the size of the segment.

*Tip*

If you drag the end of a control point outside the visible area of the screen, you see the **All** option of the **Zoom** tool to place everything in view.

*Notes*

The farther you move the control point from the node the larger the curve segment becomes.

All three primary types of nodes modify the way a curve can be moved with control points. For more information, see *Curves* and *Node Editing*.

# Converting Text To Curves

*Purpose*

Enables you to use all of CorelDraw's curve manipulation capabilities on text strings. Use this command to change a character's shape or to modify an existing font to make a logo. Remember that after you use this command, the object is a series of combined curves and cannot be treated as text.

*To convert text to curves*

1. Select the **Pick** tool from the Toolbox.

2. Click once on the target text block.

3. From the **Arrange** menu, select **Convert To Curves**.

The block is now a combined curved object and can be modified with the Shape tool or any other bezier-based command.

### Keyboard Shortcut

Select the text block with the Pick tool, and press Alt-A-V.

### Notes

Make sure that you set any options in the Text Entry and Character Attributes dialog boxes before converting the text into curves. After the change is made, it cannot be undone unless you immediately use the Undo command.

If you plan to convert only part of a text string, make two separate objects with the Text tool. This procedure limits the number of letters you must convert to curves.

You must separate any characters that overlap so that they can be filled or outlined. Use the Zoom tool to magnify the area and then use the Shape tool to separate the individual letters.

Text that has been converted to curves is not treated as fonts by Postscript printers.

# Copying Objects

### Purpose

Places a copy of an object or group of objects in the Windows Clipboard. The copy can be moved to another Windows application for further use, or pasted back into the same CorelDraw illustration.

### To copy an object

1. Select the Pick tool from the Toolbox.

2. Select the object you want to copy.

   To copy several objects, use a Marquee Selection box.

3. From the **Edit** menu, select **Copy**.

### Keyboard Shortcut

With the **Pick** tool, select the object or objects and press **Ctrl-Insert**.

### Tip

You can copy radial fills within CorelDraw by using the Place Duplicate command.

### Notes

Bitmaps and Postscript fills cannot be placed in the Clipboard from CorelDraw. Problems often develop when you try to copy an object that contains a radial fill.

An object that is too complicated cannot be pasted into CorelDraw from the Clipboard, even if it was taken from CorelDraw.

Use this command to move objects between Windows programs such as Ami Professional, CorelDraw, and Microsoft Word for Windows. Using Copy may be quicker than using the Import option for moving an object from an existing Corel file to another. See *Place Duplicate*.

# Copy Style From

### Purpose

Copies style settings from one object to another object or group of objects. With this command, you can set the fill, outline color, outline pen, text attributes (text only), or any combination of these options.

### To copy style settings

1. Select the **Pick** tool from the Toolbox.

2. If you plan to copy to several objects, do the following:

   • Draw a Marquee Selection box around the objects, or use the **Shift-Click** method to select the target objects.

   • From the **Edit** menu, select **Group**.

3. Select the source object with the **Pick** tool.

4. Verify those style attributes you want copied by opening the appropriate tools or dialog boxes.

5. From the **Edit** menu, select **Copy Style From**.

6. Click on the options listed that you want copied to the target object or objects.

7. Click **OK** when you finish making the selections.

   The Copy Style dialog box disappears and the cursor becomes a large arrow containing the word From?.

8. Click on the object or group of objects you want changed.

   The Copy Style cursor remains on-screen until you make a selection and return to the Pick tool.

*Keyboard shortcut*

Select the source object and press **Alt-E-S**.

# Curves

*Purpose*

Creates many of the shapes used in CorelDraw drawings. CorelDraw uses Bezier curves. Bezier curves are named after the French mathematician who invented them. Although you needn't know the inner workings of Bezier curves, to effectively use CorelDraw it is a good idea to practice with them.

CorelDraw considers any line that is not a straight line to be a curve. Curves follow one set of rules, and lines another. You can convert a line to a curve and make a curve a line (see *Editing Curves* ).

A straight line is created by clicking the mouse button once at the beginning of the line, moving the mouse to the end of the line, and clicking again. Any line drawn while dragging the mouse or with the Convert to Curves command, no matter how straight, is a curve in CorelDraw. A curved object in CorelDraw can contain segments that are straight lines.

### To see and edit the parts of a curve

1. Select the Shape tool from the Toolbox.

2. Place the point of the wedge-shaped cursor on the object, and click the mouse.

   A series of small squares called nodes appears. Attached to each node is one or more control points.

### Notes

This procedure does not work with bitmaps, straight lines, or text that has not been converted to curves.

As you work with curves, the Status Line indicates the type and number of nodes selected. Use this information so that you know exactly how a given segment will behave.

You must understand a few terms before you can effectively use curves. The following section covers the names and functions of the different parts and attributes of a curve.

| | |
|---|---|
| Closed Path | The object has no open aspects and can be filled (opposite of an Open path). If a Closed Object is broken open, the fill disappears. |
| Control Point | The little black boxes at the end of the dashed lines coming out of a node. Control points can be pulled or moved by dragging the mouse to change the shape of the curve. The exact number and operation of a |

control point depends on the type of node and segment involved.

Cusp Node
A node with two control points that can move independently, which enables you to make sharp and extreme changes in the shape of the curve.

First Node
The hollow box that shows its location a little larger than the other nodes. Signifies where the curve begins.

Launch Angle
The angle at which the control points of a node intersect. It effects the way the curve is shaped.

Node
A point on a curve that denotes the beginning or end of a segment. By manipulating nodes or their control points, you can modify the shape of the object. A curved object passes through a series (at least two and maybe thousands) of nodes. Because nodes do not have to be connected, one object may contain several types of nodes.

Open Path
A curve that is not closed and cannot be filled. You can use the Shape tool to close the open section or combine it with another curve or line to allow it to be filled.

Segment
The part of a curve that lies between two nodes. You can change the style of a segment from a straight line or curve, and add or delete nodes to increase or decrease its relative size.

Subpath
A series of connected segments forming all or part of a curved

object. A curved object may be broken up into several subpaths. Subpaths do not have to appear to be physically connected. This object may look as if it is several different objects, but a change in the outline will modify all segments.

Smooth Node    The node and both its control points are in a straight line. You may move the control points independently, but the other control point adapts to keep the curve for both segments smooth.

Symmetrical    The Control Points are on a
Node           straight line and must be the same distance from the node. Any change made to one point shifts the other point exactly the same distance.

# Cut

*Purpose*

Removes an object from the current drawing and places it in the Windows Clipboard. The object can be saved (from the Clipboard) or pasted into another Windows application.

*To cut an object from the current drawing*

1. Select the Pick Tool.

2. Click on the target object.

3. From the Edit menu, select Cut.

The object is now on the Clipboard.

### Keyboard Shortcut

With the Pick tool, select the target object and press Shift-Del.

### Notes

You cannot cut or copy objects containing Postscript or Radial fills to the Clipboard. To export these options, save the file using the Export command.

Limitations do exist and vary depending on the combination of Windows and CorelDraw that you are using. See the Corel Technical Reference or the Windows User Guide for more information.

# Drawing Freehand Curves

### Purpose

Creates curves or a combination of curves. Objects created with this method (no matter how straight) technically are not lines, but can be combined with lines to form complex objects. These objects may take any shape, and can be edited as a Bezier object. Objects that have a closed path can be filled using the Outline tool.

### To draw freehand curves

1. Select the Freehand tool.

2. Place the mouse at the starting point for your new object.

3. Drag the mouse as you draw the object. You can move the mouse in any direction, and the curve follows your movements.

4. Release the mouse button.

   To draw additional objects, repeat Steps 2 through 4.

## Notes

You can draw a straight line using the steps outlined in the next entry, and use Auto-Join to combine them into one element with a curved object.

Adjust how tightly the mouse conforms to your actions by setting the Freehand Tracking option in the Preferences menu. Lower settings result in closer (and possibly more jagged) results. Settings range from 1 to 10. Higher settings produce a smoother curve. The proper setting depends on the task at hand.

If you draw several objects at the same time that start and end within the Auto-Join limit, they will become one object. If the result is a Closed Path, it can be filled.

# Drawing Lines

## Purpose

Creates a straight line or group of lines using the mouse. These objects are not curves but can be combined with curves to form complex objects.

## To draw a line

1. Select the Freehand tool.

2. Place the mouse at the starting point for your new object.

3. Click once with the mouse.

   Move the mouse in any direction, and a straight line follows your movements.

4. Position the mouse at the desired end point of the line.

5. Click the mouse button.

   To draw additional objects, repeat Steps 2 through 4.

## *Notes*

The Grid does not have any effect on the Freehand tool, no matter how it is set.

The Status Line tells you the length of the x- and y-axis, the length of the line, and its direction.

If you draw several objects at the same time that start and end within the Auto-Join limit, they will become one object. If the result is a Closed Path, it can be filled.

Holding the Constrain Key will limit the line to vertical, horizontal, or a multiple of the 15-degree angle.

# Edit Text

## *Purpose*

Changes the letters in a block of text that has been placed on the page, or changes the character attributes for an entire text string.

## *To edit a block of text*

1. Choose the **Select** tool from the Toolbox.

2. Click on the text block you want to edit.

3. From the **Edit** menu, select **Edit Text**.

   The Text dialog box is displayed, and you see the blinking cursor in the Text Entry Box.

4. Modify any text.

   You also can change any of the following options:

   - Alignment (click on the desired radio button)

   - Font (click on the new font from the selection box)

   - Point Size (type the value or use the arrows)

   - Style (click on the appropriate radio button)

If you want to change the spacing, click on the command button below the Font Selection box. The Text Spacing dialog box provides the following options:

- Inter-Word spacing

- Inter-Character spacing

- Inter-Line spacing

Click OK to return to the preceding dialog box.

4. Click OK to make the changes or Cancel to abandon the changes.

### Keyboard Shortcut

Select the text block with the Pick tool and press Ctrl-T.

### Notes

Windows 3 users must press Ctrl-Enter or Ctrl-M to place a hard line return in the Text Entry box.

The Text Entry box has a limit of 250 characters. If you want to create a larger block, you must create a second text object. (See the *Text* entry in this book.)

You cannot use the Group command with Edit Text.

Use the Character Attributes (see the listing in this book) to change settings of only some of the characters in a string.

# Editing Curves/Lines

### Purpose

Redefines the basic form of the object. Depending on the nature of the object, it will have a number of control points and nodes that you can modify.

### To move a node or nodes (stretch and move a segment)

1. Select the Shape tool from the Toolbox.

2. Click on the node you want to edit. If you want to edit more than one node, use the Shift-Click method or draw a Marquee Selection box.

   The nodes and control points will now be visible, and the Status Line will indicate the type of object and the number of nodes.

3. Place the Shape tool on the desired node and drag it to the new position.

   As you drag the node, the Status Line shows the x- and y-axis size, along with the total length and angle of the segment.

4. Release the mouse button.

   If you move a node, the control points for that node move with it, and the angles remain the same. To change the angle, adjust the control points.

### To adjust the angle, shape, or length of a segment using control points

1. Select the Shape tool.

2. Click on the node involved.

   The node changes to black, and the control points become visible.

3. Drag the black box at the end of the dashed line to reshape the angle.

   The Status Line displays the x- and y-axis size, total length, and the angle of the segment you are manipulating with the control point.

   The exact movement and range of motion depends on the type of node and the adjacent segments.

### To add, delete, join, break, or change the type of a node or segment

1. Select the Shape tool from the Toolbox.

2. Double-click directly on the node or segment you want to modify.

The node or segment turns black, and the Node Edit menu is displayed. The Status Line shows the current type.

3. Click on the menu selection you want as the new value or click **Cancel** to abandon the operation.

### Notes

You can use the preceding methods to edit objects created with the Rectangle, Ellipse, and Text tools only after you use the Convert To Curves command from the Arrange menu. You cannot edit bitmap objects with these commands.

Use the Character Attributes command to change attributes of individual characters in a text string. Using the Constrain key as you move nodes or control points limits the motion to perfectly horizontal and vertical directions.

If you do not see a control point on a node, it may be hidden under the node or the curve.

If the control point you want to move is underneath a node, click the Shape tool on an unused area, press and hold the **Shift** key as you drag the mouse to move the control point. This procedure automatically selects that node.

For more details on types of nodes and segments, see *Curves* and *Node Edit*.

# Export

### Purpose

Provides the capability to save your work in a variety of both vector and bitmap file formats for use in other programs. Each format has advantages and disadvantages. The best choice depends on such factors as the final use of the illustration, target program, type of output device (printer, typesetter, slide maker, etc.), file size, the types of fills, and the use of color. Each successive release of CorelDraw has improved and added to the export capability.

## *To export a file*

1. Open the File menu with any tool.

2. Select the Save or Save As option to make a CDR CorelDraw copy of your work.

3. From the File menu, select **Export**.

   The Export Dialog box appears.

4. Select the format you want from the selection box.

   Scroll with the arrows to see additional file types.

5. Select from the following options by clicking on the radio buttons and checkboxes:

   | | |
   |---|---|
   | Selected Objects | Enables you to write only the parts of the drawing that were selected when the Export option was chosen. |
   | Include All Artistic Attributes | Increases the accuracy of complicated drawings in some formats. It often requires more disk space. |
   | Include Image Header | Places a bitmap copy of the drawing in an Encapsulated Postscript (EPS) file. In some programs, you can see and edit the image. |
   | All Fonts Resident | Speeds the eventual printing of the file with a Postscript printer if all fonts are resident or already downloaded. If a font is not present, it may not print at all if this option is selected. |
   | Resolution | Applies to the PCX and TIF bitmap selections, and enables you to set the number of pixels per inch from 40 to 300 in four steps. |

Fixed Size          Limits the dot pattern of the
                    TIF header file in an EPS
                    export.

Only the active selections for that file type are
available. The rest appear grayed out.

6. Click OK to confirm your choices.

   The Export File Selection box appears, and the
   export file type is shown on the top line.

7. Make selections for additional dialog boxes that
   relate to specific export formats. For more
   information see the sub-entries below.

8. Type the name and set the path for your new file.

9. Click OK to save the file.

   Follow the preceding steps and then do the
   following for these export procedures:

### To export a file to the Adobe Illustrator AI format

10. Choose to send text as text or as curves by clicking
    on the associated radio button from the Export AI
    dialog box that appears after performing Step 9.

    Generally choose as text if the fonts will match
    those in Adobe Illustrator. If you are using other
    fonts, have edited individual character attributes,
    or have any text that was set using the Corel Fit
    Text To Path command, export with the Send Text
    as Curves option.

11. Click OK on the command button.

    Use AI to export to Macintosh programs that use
    this type of file and cannot use EPS exports.
    While it is a subset of Encapsulated Postscript, it
    does not support many of CorelDraw's more
    advanced text and fill features.

### To export a file to the AutoCAD DXF format

This export filter only provides the outlines of the
drawing, including text objects.

### *To export a file to the Artline GEM format*

GEM file types vary, and all have limited capabilities in relation to color, fills, and the complexity of objects. They do not allow bitmapped data as part of the drawing. For more information see the CorelDraw Technical Reference.

### *To export a file to the Computer Graphics Metafile CGM format*

There are no extra steps required to export CGM files, but you should probably make use of the Include All Artistic Attributes option if you have fountain fills in the drawing. This CGM format is not currently compatible with WordPerfect or Harvard Graphics.

### *To export a file to the Encapsulated Postscript (EPS) format*

If you want to use the Corel image in another program in conjunction with a Postscript device, choose EPS. If you include the Header file, you can see a sample of the image, which you can position and crop. If you don't include the Header file, you cannot see the image.

### *To export a file to the Hewlett Packard Graphics Language PLT Plotter Format (Outlines Only)*

10. Select the desired options in the Export HPGL Outline dialog box, which appears after you finish Step 9 of the general instructions. The choices include:

- Scale factors, for horizontal and vertical stretching
- Pen Velocity in centimeters per second
- Curve Resolution
- Color/Pen Selection
- Export only the selected color

11. Click **OK** to save the export file, **Reset** to return to Corel's default values, or **Cancel** to abort the operation.

HPGL export enables you to send files to an HP or compatible plotter, or use the files in a program that supports such devices.

You cannot export bitmaps, complex fills, textures, or calligraphic effects through this filter.

### To export a file to the IBM PIF (GDF) format

This export filter can be used to transfer Corel artwork to IBM mainframes. The result will be full size, and can be edited on the host computer with the proper software.

### To export a file to the Macintosh PICT format

Use this option to move any Corel art, except bitmapped portions, to an Apple Macintosh. Color is limited by the type of Mac system being used. It is generally a good idea to select Include All Artistic Attributes in the Export dialog box.

### To export a file to the Publishers' Paintbrush ZSoft PCX format

Files are stored as a collection of black and white dots and can be edited in many paint programs. CorelDraw does not have a feature to incorporate color or gray-scale data in bitmap exports, but aside from this limitation it is probably the best choice for desktop publishers who do not have Postscript capability.

### To export a file to the Tagged Image File Format, TIF

This format has the same limits and capabilities as Paintbrush PCX. Both PageMaker and Ventura Publisher can use these files, but the EPS format is better for users with Postscript printers.

Large bitmaps can use a lot of disk space and are prone to the "jaggies." For both reasons it is a good idea to make the image the size you need as a finished product before exporting.

### To export a file to the VideoShow PIC format

This format can be used by some new display and publishing packages as well as for creating slides and presentations with VideoShow hardware.

If you are using VideoShow, make sure that your first picture for the presentation has a white or black background. Failure to do that may confuse the software.

For 35mm slides set the CorelDraw page size to a 12 by 8 ratio, which matches the aspect ratio of a slide's active area.

For more information on using this export option, consult the presentation system's hardware and software as well as the CorelDraw Technical Reference.

### To export a file to the WordPerfect WPG format

10. Choose the number of colors (16 or 256) from the EXPORT WPG Selection Box that appears after entering the export file name.

11. Click OK. The box disappears and the file will be written to disk.

Be sure to set any rotations in CorelDraw and within WordPerfect for files exported with this option.

Bitmap objects, Postscript Textures, and complex fills are not supported.

Text in the drawing cannot be edited in WordPerfect because it has been converted to curves. Make sure you make any corrections to your text before exporting.

### Tip

Always save a copy of a file to be exported in the native CDR (CorelDraw) format before exporting. It is a good idea to test the quality of the export for critical work and complex objects or fills. The result varies from system to system and drawing to drawing. The EPS and PCX formats give the overall best results in most cases.

# Fill

## Purpose

All closed objects that are part of a Corel drawing have two components: the outline, or outer boundary, and the fill, or inner area. An object must be closed before you can apply a fill. You cannot apply fill to open paths or straight lines. Corel provides a host of fill options that include process and spot color, shades of gray, radial or linear fountain fills, uniform fills, halftone patterns, and Postscript textures.

## To define a default fill for the Fill tool

1. With no object selected, select the Fill tool.

   The Fill flyout menu appears.

2. Select the desired icon, such as the paintbucket or shade of gray.

   The New Object Uniform Fill dialog box appears.

3. Click OK to reset the default value or Cancel to abandon the operation.

4. Set the values for the desired fill, and exit from any dialog boxes.

The following sections explain the options you can choose as you work with fills.

## To set black, white, none, or one of the preset gray fills for an existing object or group of objects

1. With any tool, open the Display menu if the Preview window is visible.

   Proceed to Step 3 if the Display menu is open.

2. Select Show Preview to see the available fills.

3. Select the Pick or Shape tool from the Toolbox.

4. Click on the target object you want filled, or use the Shift-Click or Marquee Selection method for a group of objects.

5. Select the Fill tool from the Toolbox.

   The Fill flyout menu appears.

6. Select one of the following fill values that appear to the right of the paintbucket: None, White, Black, and 10, 20, 40, 60, 80 percent gray.

   The Flyout menu disappears and the fill is set.

### To create a custom uniform gray, process, or spot color fill

1. With any tool, open the Display menu.

   Proceed to Step 3 if the Display menu is open.

2. Select Show Preview to see the result.

3. Select the Pick or Shape tool from the Toolbox.

4. Click on the target object you want filled, or use the Shift-Click or Marquee Selection method for a group of objects.

5. Select the Fill tool from the Toolbox.

   The Fill flyout menu appears.

6. Choose the Paintbucket icon, which is on the left side of the flyout menu.

   The flyout is replaced with the Uniform Fill dialog box.

7. Select Spot or Process color.

8. Click OK.

   The appropriate options are displayed.

9. To set a shade of gray, adjust the Tint or Black value by entering a number in the Color Entry box via the keyboard or clicking the arrows to the right of the box.

   The color you select is displayed in the box to the left of the dialog box.

Follow these instructions for the option you selected:

If you selected Spot color, complete the following steps:

10. Set the Color value by entering a number in the Color entry box via the keyboard or using the

arrows to the right of the box. If you want to use a specific PANTONE color, place that number in the box.

The color you select is displayed in the box to the left of the dialog box, and the name or number of the color is displayed beneath the box.

11. Set the **Tint** value by entering a number in the Tint entry box via the keyboard, or using the arrows to the right of the box. This setting adjusts the amount of black in the color, making it lighter or darker. Zero is white and 100 is black.

12. If you are using a Postscript output device, select **Postscript**.

13. Set the **Type** (shape) of the halftone pattern.

14. Set the **Frequency** of the lines per inch.

15. Set the **Angle** of the pattern in degrees.

16. Click **OK** to confirm or **Cancel** to abandon the Postscript Halftone.

If you selected **Process** color, complete the following steps:

10. Use the arrows or keyboard to set the combination of primary colors (**Cyan**, **Magenta**, **Yellow**, and **Black**) that yield the exact color you want.

The color you select is displayed in the box to the left of the entry box.

11. Click **OK** to confirm or **Cancel** to abandon your work.

12  Click **OK**.

### To create a custom fountain fill

1. With any tool, open the **Display** menu if the Preview window is not visible. Proceed to Step 3 if the Display menu is open.

2. Select **Show Preview** to see the fills.

3. Select the **Pick** or **Shape** tool from the Toolbox.

4. Click on the target object you want filled, or use the Shift-Click or Marquee Selection method for a group of objects.

5. Select the Fill tool from the Toolbox.

   The Fill flyout menu appears.

6. Click on the next to the last icon (starburst) on the flyout menu.

   The menu is replaced with the Fountain Fill dialog box.

7. Select the radial or linear radio button.

   If you select linear, set the angle of the fill.

Follow these instructions for the option you selected:

If you selected Spot color, complete the following steps:

8. Set the Color for both the From and To options by entering a number in both entry boxes via the keyboard or using the arrows to the right of the box. If you want to use specific PANTONE colors, place the numbers in the boxes.

   The color you select is displayed in the box to the left of the entry boxes, and the name or number of the colors appears beneath the box.

9. Set the Tint values for both From and To options by entering a number in the Tint entry boxes via the keyboard or using the arrows to the right of the boxes. This setting adjusts the amount of black in the colors, making them lighter or darker. 0 is white and 100 is black.

If you selected Process color, complete the following steps:

10. Use the arrows or keyboard to set the combination of primary colors (Cyan, Magenta, Yellow, and Black) that yield the exact color you want.

    The color you select is displayed in the box to the left of the entry box.

11. Click OK to confirm or Cancel to abandon your work.

12. If you are using a Postscript output device, select Postscript.

13. Set the Type (shape) of the halftone pattern.

14. Set the Frequency of the lines per inch.

15. Set the Angle of the pattern in degrees.

16. Click OK to confirm or Cancel to abandon the Postscript Halftone.

17. Click OK or Cancel in the primary Spot Color Dialog box.

### Notes

All closed objects in CorelDraw have a fill setting, even if the value is None. The None option is transparent and lets the object below show through the fill area.

The Status Line indicates the color or shade of fill for a selected object.

PANTONE colors may not exactly match the one shown in the PANTONE Color Guide. This discrepancy is due to variations in display screens. Use the guide as a reference in choosing a color.

The Linear Fountain Fills direction is set by the angle from which the fill begins. A compass rose is shown in the dialog box as a reference.

If you are using a Postscript printer, you can print separate pages for each of the colors set in Process color.

If at all possible, use the same type of color model, spot or process, for all fills in the same CorelDraw file. If you are planning to export your work, make sure that the type of fill you are using is supported by that format.

See also *Spot and Process Color* and *Postscript Textures*.

# Fit Text To Path

### Purpose

Makes text flow around a circle or almost any shape imaginable. Precise placement of the text on the path is determined by a combination of the way the path object was created and the alignment setting used when the text was entered.

### *To flow text around an object*

1. Use the appropriate tool and commands to create the path object.

   You can use almost any object, including a text element. The method you use to create the object and text affects the final result.

2. If the path object is a text character, use the Convert To Curves command on the path object only (not the text to be fitted).

3. Using the Text tool, enter the text.

4. Select the Pick tool from the Toolbox.

5. Select both the path object and text object using either the Shift-Click method or a Marquee Selection box.

6. From the Arrange menu, select Fit Text To Path.

   You can delete the path object at this point without effecting the new shape of the text.

### *Tip*

Select the final font before you fit the text to the path. Changing the font or using the Edit Text or Character Attributes commands can shift the relationship of text to the target object.

### *Notes*

Where the text is placed depends on the way the path object was drawn, and how the text is aligned. Text is fitted in the direction the object is drawn for curves and lines. From left to right places the text above the object, and right to left places it below the object.

For objects created with the Ellipse or Rectangle tools the following rules apply:

• Drag up and right or down and left to place the path on the outside.

- Drag down and right or up and left to place the path on the inside of the object.

The place at which the text begins on the path is set by how it is aligned in the Text dialog box. You can choose the following:

- Left or None results in the text being placed at the start of the path.

- Center alignment centers the text in the path.

- Right alignment sets the end of the text string at the end of the path.

To place the fitted text on the top center of a circle, draw the circle from the lower left to the upper right, and set the text alignment to Center.

If you have an unexpected result, use the Mirror function to reverse the result, or use Straighten Text to return the text to normal.

Always use text that appears in a straight line for the Fit Text To Path command.

Fit Text To Path cannot be used to fit text to objects that are grouped together. The command works with objects that are combined, but the fit follows the path of the "new" combined object.

# Fonts

### Purpose

A font is a specific style and size of a given typeface, such as Helvetica or Times Roman. CorelDraw comes with more than 43 typefaces, some of which can be used in italic, bold, and bold italic variations. The CorelTypeface Reference Chart shows the fonts that are packaged with the software. Although the font names may not be familiar, they are similar, if not identical, to familiar typefaces. Appendix C of the CorelDraw Users' manual provides a conversion list.

## *To change the names of Corel fonts*

1. Load a word processor or text editor that can handle an ASCII (text) file.

2. Make a backup copy of the WIN.INI file (located in the Windows directory) named **WIN.OLD**.

3. Open the original WIN.INI file.

4. Locate the part of the file that begins `[CorelDrwFonts]`.

5. Change the names of the fonts that are in front of the equal (=) sign to the name you want. Do not delete the equal sign or change any part of the following text. Do not use any spaces in the names of the fonts. You can use the Underscore key to show the break between two words, such as **Times_Roman**.

6. Save the file as WIN.INI in ASCII text format.

7. Reload Windows.

   If you encounter any problems, change the name of WIN.OLD to **WIN.INI**.

## *To change the sample in the Text Entry dialog box*

1. With any tool, open the **Special** menu.

2. Select **Preferences**.

3. Click on the **Typeface Selection Char** option entry box.

4. Type the character you want to appear in the box.

5. Click **OK**.

## *Note*

Font names cannot contain spaces, and a name must be no more than 24 characters long.

# Font Conversion

## Purpose

Enables you to use the Wfn BOSS utility, which is included with CorelDraw, so that you can use fonts from a variety of vendors within Corel. Wfn BOSS automatically installs when you place CorelDraw on your hard disk.

The utility works with Adobe Type 1, Agfa Compugraphic, Bitstream, Digifont, Readable Postscript, ZSoft Type Foundry, and printer-resident Postscript fonts. In addition, WFN BOSS can create a version of Corel's fonts that can be exported to Publisher's Type Foundry and customized.

## To use fonts from other vendors

1. Load Windows.

2. With the mouse, double-click on the **WFN BOSS** icon. (The icon has a capital A and an arrow pointing to a cartoon face of a man with a mustache.)

   The WFN BOSS screen appears.

3. Click the checkbox next to the font you want to convert.

4. Change to the directory in which the source fonts are located using the NEW DIR button, if necessary.

5. If you want to place the fonts in a different directory, change the Destination Directory listing.

6. In the Available Fonts selection box, select the name of the font you want to convert.

   The New Font Data box turns from gray to black and provides default settings.

7. Change any of these settings:

   - **Font Weight**
   - **CorelDraw Name**
   - **File Name**

8. Set any of the following options from the Options menu:

- **Font File Info** provides a font listing and changes the default character and Postscript Invocation Name.
- **AutoInstall** updates the WIN.INI file after the conversion is complete.
- **Compress Fonts** is used for readable Postscript.
- **Convert All** converts all fonts on the active list (up to 32) at once.

9. Select **Convert**.

The Status and Prompts box advises you of operations as they are performed.

### Notes

Use WFN BOSS's AutoInstall option if you reinstall CorelDraw with a newer version or path. Information about any fonts you converted in the past are kept in a special file and can be updated without going through the entire process.

An extensive Help menu provides detailed information on options and font formats.

# Grid

### Purpose

Draws and positions objects to exact size. To make proper use of this feature, set the Grid Size and activate the Snap To Grid option. Because Grid Units are saved with drawings, they are available when you modify an illustration. Unlike some draw programs, the Corel grid is invisible.

### To set the grid unit

1. With any tool, select the **Display** menu.

2. Select **Grid Size**.

The Grid dialog box appears.

3. Choose from these units of measure: **inches**, **centimeters**, **picas**, or **points**.

4. Set the Grid Frequency by entering a number or using the arrows. You can enter decimal values.

5. Click **OK** to confirm or **Cancel** to abandon the operation.

### Keyboard Shortcuts

**Alt-D-Z** toggles the Snap To Grid feature.

or

With any tool select the **Display** menu. An arrow to the left of the Snap To Grid option indicates that it is active. If you want to change the option, click once. To reverse your choice, click again.

Press **F6** or **Alt-D-G** to toggle Snap To Grid on and off.

### Notes

Objects move or are drawn in units equal to the size of the Grid except in the following instances. The Grid never limits use of the Freehand tool, selecting an object, using the Copy Style Command, Rotating and Skewing with the Pick Tool, or the use of the Zoom function.

You can override the Grid at any time by using the Constrain (Control) key during an operation.

The Grid Frequency setting also is the unit of measure for the optional CorelDraw Rulers.

# Group/Ungroup

### Purpose

Enables you to join several objects together so that they act as a single element. The objects do not have to touch, and operations such as Fill or Outline modify each member of the group. This command is not the same as Combine.

### *To group objects*

1. Select the Pick tool from the Toolbox.

2. Use either the Shift-Click or Marquee Selection method to mark the objects you want to group.

3. From the Arrange menu, select Group.

### *To ungroup an existing group*

Follow the preceding steps, but select Ungroup.

### *Keyboard Shortcuts*

Alt-A-G groups objects. Alt-A-U ungroups objects.

### *Notes*

You can use the Marquee Selection box to temporarily group objects. The objects ungroup when you click on a blank area.

You can move, rotate, scale, outline, and fill groups as if the members are a single object.

Combine and Group are mutually exclusive. You must deactivate one before choosing the other. As long as a set of objects is defined as a group you cannot select individual objects.

You cannot use the Shape tool on a group, change the option to Combine to edit curves or ungroup the set.

You cannot record a macro using a group as the target.

Align to Baseline, Edit Text, Fit Text To Path, and Straighten Text Commands do not work on text that is part of a group.

# Halftones

### *Purpose*

If you have a Postscript printer, you can adjust settings for Outline Color, Uniform, and Fountain Fills under the Spot Color option. With these settings, you gain control over the texture, angle, and frequency of the fill (including those used to print bitmaps). Halftones do not appear in the Preview window, but appear only after the drawing is printed.

## To set halftones

1. You must have one of the following dialog boxes open: Outline Color (Outline/Brush), Uniform Fill (Paintbucket), or Fountain Fill (Paintbucket/ Starburst icon).

   If you do not select an object before you set fill options, the changes made become the new program defaults.

2. Select Spot color.

   Halftones cannot be set for Process color.

3. Select Postscript after you make your other selections.

   The Postscript Halftone Screen dialog box appears.

4. Locate the desired Halftone Screen Type by scrolling through the list using the arrows.

5. Click on the type you want to use.

   You have the following choices: Dot, Dot2, Line, Diamonds, Microwave, and Outline Circles in either white or black.

6. Set the Halftone Screen Frequency by clicking on the arrows or entering the settings.

7. Set the Halftone Screen Angle by clicking on the arrows or tentering the settings.

8. Click OK to confirm your choices or Cancel to abandon the changes.

9. Click OK to exit the dialog box.

## Notes

Set the Screen Frequency for the effect you want and the resolution of the output device. A trade-off exists between the number of gray levels available and the screen lines used. A 60-line screen at 300 dpi (the default setting with a standard laser printer) yields 26 shades of gray, but the same setting results in an output of 400 dpi with a typesetter printing at 1200 dpi.

Use a coarse screen (40-65 dpi) for photocopies. For most work the CorelDraw defaults are adequate.

The Angle Setting determines the direction of the line pattern.

You can use the preset shades that appear on the flyout menu (white, black, or percent of gray) with the halftone option. Note that black or white covers the entire object.

If you choose Default, the frequency and angle setting are gray and set to 60 lines per inch at 45 degrees.

# Help

### *Purpose*

CorelDraw is packaged with several different guides that help you get the most from the program. In many cases, these guides and this Quick Reference can save the time and expense of a long distance phone call.

### *To get help on installation*

1. Read the Read Me First manual.

2. Read the Installation Procedures, which begin on page 6 of the Users' Manual (the large spiral bound book with the black cover).

3. If you are having difficulty using CorelDraw with a printer, plotter, or other peripheral device, read the section on page 54 of the CorelDraw Technical Reference.

### *To get help on program operation or tools*

1. If possible, view the video tape to see how the program functions. The tape contains good examples that are easy to understand.

2. Consult the CorelDraw Users' Manual for the specific topic.

### To get help importing or exporting files, and using CorelDraw with other programs

1. Refer to the CorelDraw Technical Reference.

2. Consult the manual of the other program to see which file formats it has in common with CorelDraw.

### To get help with CorelTrace

1. Read the small blue CorelTrace guide.

2. Sections in the Users' Manual can help you understand some of the settings, such as the racking setting in the Preferences sections.

### To get help with font converstion and fonts

1. All conversion information is contained in the WFN Boss handbook.

2. The Corel Typeface Reference chart and Appendix C of the Users' Manual contain samples of different fonts, plus the name used by Postscript for similar typefaces.

### To get help with clip art disks

1. To identify the contents and file types, refer to the Clip Art Catalog that comes with CorelDraw.

2. The Technical Reference explains the differences and capabilities of the different file formats used to create and store the images.

### To get help selecting colors for fills and outlines

1. Use the CorelDraw Process Color Reference chart.

2. You can obtain a PANTONE color numbers chart at most large art supply stores.

### *To access the CorelDraw technical assistance bulletin board*

1. Turn on your modem and load the telecommunications software.

2. Set your modem for 1200 or 2400 baud, 8 bits, 1 stop bit, and no parity.

3. Dial Corel Systems at (613) 728-4752.

   The BBS software answers. Reply to the questions.

4. You are logged on the BBS. Menus help guide you.

5. If you are uploading a file, leave a message to the SYSop to explain the file.

6. Use the Main menu Goodby option to exit the system so that you do not tie up the BBS.

   Note that the Bulletin Board has a time limit per user per day. Plan to download any files first.

# Import

### *Purpose*

Enables you to import or trace both vector and bitmap file formats created in other programs to CorelDraw as part of a drawing. Each file format has its own limitations. Experiment with the file types of the other program to see which format works best with CorelDraw. Windows applications also can trade images via the Windows Clipboard.

### *To import all except Windows Clipboard*

1. Open the File menu with the Pick tool.

2. Select Import.

   The Import dialog box appears.

3. Click on the format you want, or scroll with the arrows to see additional file types.

4. If you are importing a PCX or TIF file format to autotrace, select **For Tracing**.

   Do not use this option if you are importing a bitmap as a permanent part of the CorelDraw file because the bitmap will not print.

5. Click **OK** to confirm your choices.

   The Import File selection box is displayed, and the import file type is shown on the top line.

6. Double-click on the name of the file you want to import to CorelDraw.

*Keyboard Shortcut*

Alt-F-I

*Notes*

The hourglass wait icon may appear as the file is being imported.

Bitmap files appear at a low resolution to speed screen redraws and conserve memory. They print at full resolution.

Use the **Zoom** tool to enlarge the image and see more detail.

The following file formats are available for use with CorelDraw (early versions may not import all formats):

**CorelDraw, CDR Format**

This format is the native CorelDraw format, and is used to import clip art and images created in CorelDraw. Importing adds the image to the current drawing. This format is not the same as using the Files menu New Command, which removes the existing drawing and opens a blank page.

**CorelTrace, EPS Format**

Use the EPS format to import CorelTrace files. EPS formats are the result of converting a bitmap PCX or TIF file to a vector drawing. The image is

loaded as a group of objects with closed paths.
You can use the Ungroup command to separate
the objects into individual elements. Fill and edit
the objects as any other curves in CorelDraw. The
CorelTrace file does not contain any color
information except black and white.

### Adobe Illustrator, AI and EPS Format

Use this format to import clip art and drawings
created in Adobe Illustrator. The drawings appear
as a group of objects, which you can separate and
edit individually. The AI file format is not exactly
the same as an EPS file, although both formats are
created using the Postscript language.

### AutoCAD, DXF Format (Outlines Only)

This format has some severe limitations when
imported into non-CAD software, and CorelDraw
is no exception. If the DXF file contains much
text, nonstandard characters, three dimensional
objects, polylines, or requirements for exact
placement of lines, you will be disappointed. You
may want to export the file from a CAD program
in the CGM format (if possible).

### Computer Graphics Metafile, CGM Format

This vector format is used on all types of
computers, from PCs to mainframes. Some
imports, such as Freelance, can include color
information and, depending on the source program,
may include text that can be edited. As a rule, if a
bitmap area is included in a CGM file, that part of
the file does not appear in CorelDraw.

### GEM Format, (Artline, Gem Draw, Ventura Publisher)

Xerox Ventura Publisher creates a GEM file for
any non-GEM vector art that it uses. You can
import that file to CorelDraw. The GEM model
allows only 16 colors, and most fill patterns do not
transfer to CorelDraw. Text in a GEM file (except
that done in Artline) can be edited in CorelDraw.

## Hewlett-Packard Graphics Language, PLT Plotter Format

To import color attributes from a PLT file, the pen settings in the WIN.INI file must be correct. (For more information see the *Export* entry in this book, the CorelDraw Technical Reference, or your Windows Users' Guide.) Text comes in as the first font listed in the WIN.INI file, and only a few object types are imported with fills.

## IBM PIF, (GDF) Format

Use this import filter to transfer artwork from IBM mainframes. White objects in the original file may not appear in the Corel drawing, but do appear after you draw a colored rectangle that covers the page and move it to the back. As with some other formats, these drawings import as a group, and must be separated for individual editing.

## Lotus 1-2-3, PIC Format

Charts created in Lotus import as a group. Use the Ungroup Command to edit individual elements, if desired.

## Macintosh, PICT Format

Use this format to move drawings from an Apple Macintosh to CorelDraw, but note that any bitmap portions are deleted. Color is limited by the Macintosh software and Corel's capability to match the colors. Outlines that are filled in the Macintosh file, import as two objects in CorelDraw, one for the outline and another for the fill.

## Publishers' Paintbrush, ZSoft PCX and PCC Formats

This format is one of the more universal for bitmap files. Files are created as a collection of black and white dots, and can be edited in many paint programs. CorelDraw does not import color as color information or gray-scale data in PCX and PCC imports.

### Tagged Image File Format, TIF

Imported TIF files can contain grayscale information within CorelDraw, but not color attributes.

*Notes*

Imported TIF bitmaps with grayscale information do not appear as such on the screen, but do print properly with a Postscript output device.

If you import a bitmap image to trace, the words `For Tracing` appear on the Status Line.

Most prepared clip art imports properly in the majority of the mentioned file formats.

If you create files in another package to use in CorelDraw, read the manual for that program to see what limitations and special considerations you should take for text and color handling. The Corel Technical Reference and Users' Manual also contain useful information.

If you want to import a file in a format that Corel does not support, try a third party program such as Collage Plus, Hijaak, or try to get the file into another Windows program and move it via the Clipboard.

# Incorporating Bitmap Images

*Purpose*

Although you cannot edit portions of bitmap images inside CorelDraw, you can use the images as part of an illustration. Bitmaps can be scaled, rotated, colored as any other object, or cropped to show only a portion of the image.

*To crop a bitmap with the Shape tool*

1. Edit a bitmap that is much larger than the portion you want to use in CorelDraw in your paint program before you import it as a PCX or TIFF file. (See *Import* .)

2. Import the bitmap using the File menu with any tool selected. Do not use the For Tracing option in the Import dialog box.

3. Select the Shape tool from the Toolbox.

4. Select the bitmap you want to crop.

   Six black handle boxes appear around the object.

5. Place the cursor over the handle nearest the area you want to crop.

6. Drag the handle to cover or expose the area you want to crop or expand.

7. Repeat the operation with any other corners to obtain the desired effect.

   The bitmap cannot be enlarged or reduced with the Shape tool.

   Use the Zoom tool to increase magnification to see more detail in the bitmap image.

   The Status Line shows the percent of crop for Top, Bottom, Left, and Right.

### To color and apply a halftone bitmap image with the Outline tool

1. Import the bitmap using the File menu with any tool selected. Do not use the For Tracing option in the Import dialog box.

2. Select the Pick tool from the Toolbox.

3. Select the bitmap you want to modify.

   Six black handle boxes appear around the object.

4. Select the Outline tool from the Toolbox.

5. You can choose one of the preset shades from the second row of the flyout menu.

   or

   For more options, select the Brush tool from the flyout menu.

6. Depending on the output device you are using, you can set the following:

- Set black, white, or a gray shade with either the Spot or Process color options.

- With a Postscript printer or typesetter, you can use the Halftone screen patterns available under the Outline Spot Color options. (See *Halftone*.)

7. After you make your selections, click OK.

### *To color and apply halftone with the Fill tool to the rectangle behind a bitmap image*

1. Import the bitmap using the File menu with any tool selected. Do not use the For Tracing option in the Import dialog box.

2. Select the Pick tool from the Toolbox.

3. Select the bitmap you want to modify.

   Six black handle boxes appear around the object.

4. Select the Fill tool from the Toolbox.

5. You can choose one of the preset shades from the flyout menu.

   or

   For more options, select the Paintbucket, Fountain, or PS (Postscript Textures) options from the flyout menu.

6. Depending on the output device you are using and the type of bitmap you have, you do the following:

   - Set a black, white, or a gray shade with either the Spot or Process color options (see the appropriate Command Reference listing for more information).

   - With a Postscript printer or typesetter, you can use the Halftone screen patterns available under the Uniform Spot Color Fill options (see *Postscript Textures* for more information).

   Selecting a fill of None causes the white pixels of the bitmap to be transparent.

Fill color does not have any effect on grayscale bitmap images, but you can control grayscale pixel color and shade for both normal and grayscale bitmaps with the Outline Color settings.

## Notes

You use different settings for the bitmap and the background rectangle.

If you rotate or skew a bitmap, the image becomes grayed and you cannot see any detail. Perform any desired cropping before changing rotation or skewing the image.

Rotated or skewed bitmaps only print on a Postscript printer.

# Inserting Special Characters

## Purpose

Enables you to insert text characters that are not on your keyboard, but are available as part of a CorelDraw font. Examples include copyright and trademark symbols, as well as characters used in foreign languages.

## To insert special characters

1. Select the Text tool from the Toolbox.

2. Click in the area the text is to appear.

   The Text Entry dialog box appears.

3. Press and hold the Alt key, and then press the appropriate numeric key as listed in Appendix B of the CorelDraw Users' Guide.

4. Finish entering text.

5. Set any desired options in the Text dialog box.

6. Click OK.

### Notes

Make sure that you enter the leading zero shown as part of the special character number in the appendix.

Most, but not all, of the special characters appear in the Text entry box. All special characters appear in the working area and the Preview window.

Not all fonts contain all special characters. You may have to choose another font to place that character.

# Leave Original

### Purpose

Enables you to make a duplicate, or modify a copy of an object or group of objects and not disturb the original element. Examples include text that is to be mirrored or shadowed, and boxes used in a form.

### To leave the original as you move the duplicate with the mouse

1. Create the original object or objects, and perform all desired modifications that are to be the same in the duplicate.

2. Select the **Pick** tool from the Toolbox.

3. Place the corner of the Pick tool on the object or group of objects. (Do not place the tool on one of the square black handles.)

4. Drag the object toward the new location for the duplicate.

5. As you drag the object, press the numeric keypad plus (+) key.

6. Place the object and release the keys.

   The original object remains in the old location.

### To leave the original as you rotate or skew

1. Create the original object or objects, and perform all desired modifications that are to be the same in the duplicate.

2. Select the **Pick** tool from the Toolbox.

3. Double-click on the object or group you want to duplicate so that the handle boxes are changed to small arrows.

   You then can choose to use the mouse method or the menu method.

   If you are using a mouse, do the following steps:

4. Place the cursor over one of the arrows and drag in the desired direction.

5. As you drag the object, press the numeric keypad plus (+) key.

6. Place the object and release the keys.

   The original object remains in the old location.

   If you are using the menu method, do the following steps:

4. From the **Transform** menu, select **Rotate and Skew**.

5. Click on the **Leave Original** checkbox.

6. Set the values for the degree of rotation or skew desired.

7. Click **OK** to confirm the operation or **Cancel** to abandon it.

### *To stretch or mirror an object*

1. Create the original object and perform all desired modifications that are to be the same in the duplicate.

2. Select the **Pick** tool from the Toolbox.

3. Click on the object you want to duplicate so that the handle boxes are visible.

   You then can choose to use the mouse method or the menu method.

   If you are using a mouse, do the following:

4. Place the cursor over one of the handles and drag in the desired direction.

5. As you drag the object, press the numeric keypad plus (+) key.

6. Place the object and release the keys.

   The original object remains in the old location.

If you are using the menu method, do the following:

4. From the Transform menu, select Stretch and Mirror.

5. Click on the Leave Original checkbox.

6. Type the values for the degree of Horizontal or Vertical stretch, or or use the arrows to change the values.

7. To mirror the object, click on either or both of the Horizontal and Vertical mirror command buttons to set the appropriate stretch value to -100%.

8. Click OK to confirm the operation or Cancel to abandon it.

---

*Notes*

If you want to duplicate a group of objects, remember that the objects must be defined as a group before you press the + key.

Using the appropriate dialog box enables you to set a precise amount of outset when using duplicates to create shadow effects.

When you use the mouse to stretch, mirror, rotate, and skew objects, the Status Line gives you a readout of the amount of change being made.

Press the Constrain key as you stretch and scale to limit the operation to 100 percent increments. This procedure is a handy way to get a mirror image of the original object when you are leaving a copy of the original.

# Lines

### Purpose

One of the most common objects in a drawing is a simple line. CorelDraw enables you quickly to form and edit perfectly straight lines and convert them to curves.

### To draw a straight line

1. Select the Freehand tool from the Toolbox.

2. Position the thin cross-shaped cursor at the point the line is to begin.

3. Click and release the mouse button once.

4. Move the mouse to the end point of the new line.

   You see a temporal line pulled as you move the mouse.

5. Click the mouse once again to finalize the line's end point.

### To draw a series of connected lines

1. Select the Freehand tool from the Toolbox.

2. Position the thin cross-shaped cursor at the point the first line is to begin.

3. Click and release the mouse button once.

4. Move the mouse to the end point of the new line.

   You see a temporary line as a guide as you move the mouse.

5. Click the mouse once again to finalize the object's end point.

6. Click the mouse once close to or on the end of the line you just created.

7. Move the mouse to the end point of the new line.

8. Click once again with the mouse.

## Notes

Objects that are open, such as simple straight lines, cannot be filled unless they become part of a closed path. You can combine any combination of lines and curves to make a closed object and then apply fills.

The thickness, ends, and pattern of a line can be modified with the Outline tool (see *Outline Attributes*).

A line can be converted into a curve with the Shape tool (see *Curves* and *Node Editing* ).

# Linear/Radial (Fountain) Fills

## Purpose

Enables you to blend two colors or shades inside a closed object. The Linear Fill can darken as it moves across the object in any direction. The Radial Fill darkens in a circular pattern from either the inside or the outside. The effect can be quite dramatic or subtle.

## To use Linear Fill

1. Select the Pick tool or Shape tool from the Toolbox.

2. Select the target closed object or objects (including bitmaps) by clicking once with the mouse.

3. Select on the Fill tool.

   A flyout menu appears.

4. Select Fountain Fill.

5. Click on the Linear Fill radio button.

6. Set the desired angle degree for the direction of fill by entering the number or clicking with the arrows.

7. Select Spot or Process color.

   For Spot color, enter the color number and tint (percent of black) for both the From and To options.

For Process color, set the Cyan, Magenta, Yellow, and Black combinations for both the From and To options.

8. If you choose Spot color and have a Postscript printer, you can select Postscript and set the type, frequency, and angle of the halftone screen.

9. Click OK to confirm your choice or Cancel to abandon the operation.

### To use Radial Fill

1. Select the Pick tool or Shape tool from the Toolbox.

2. Select the target closed object or objects (including bitmaps).

3. Select the Fill tool.

   A flyout menu appears.

4. Select Fountain Fill.

5. Click on the Radial Fill radio button.

6. Select Spot or Process color.

   For Spot color, enter the color number and tint (percent of black) for both the From and To options.

   For Process color, set the Cyan, Magenta, Yellow, and Black combinations for both the From and To options.

7. If you choose Spot color and have a Postscript printer, you can select Postscript and set the type, frequency, and angle of the halftone screen.

8. Click OK to confirm or Cancel to abandon the operation.

### To shift the visual center of a Radial Fill

The Radial Fill is oriented from the center of a circle, even if the object is not circular. To shift the position of the highligh, do the following steps:

1. Select the Freehand tool from the Toolbox.

2. Draw a short straight line with no outline color or shade from the edge of the radial filled object toward one of the object's handles.

3. Select the **Pick** tool from the Toolbox.

4. Select both the objects with the Shift-Click method or the Marquee Selection method.

5. From the **Arrange** menu, select **Combine**.

6. Select the **Shape** tool from the Toolbox.

7. Use the **Shape** tool to rotate the new line portion and reposition the center point of the radial fill. The line portion can be moved to any length and angle—even inside or through the radial filled object.

   The relative size of the radial fill circles shifts.

8. Use the Preview window to observe the changes.

### Notes

An alternate way to change the appearance of a radial fill is to use a mask to cover portions of the object.

See also *Postscript Halftones*, and S*pot Color and Process Color*.

# Macros

### Purpose

Automates a series of repetitive actions. This feature can save time and insure accuracy by letting the computer do more of the work.

### To record a macro

1. Select the **Pick** tool from the Toolbox.

2. Click on a single target object on which to base the macro.

3. With the **Pick** tool, open the **Special** menu.

4. Select Record Macro.

5. Perform the steps you want the macro to perform.

6. From the Special menu, select Finish Macro.

7. Enter a name for the macro in the File Selection box that appears.

8. Click OK to confirm the operation or choose Cancel to abort the entire macro recording.

### To play a macro

1. Select the Pick tool from the Toolbox.

2. Click once on the target object or group.

3. From the Special menu, select Play Macro.

4. Double-click on the name of the macro file you want to play.

5. Observe the final result in the Preview window.

### Note

If you try to use a macro on a group of objects and have difficulty; try breaking the group and performing the macro on the objects one at a time.

# Marquee Select

### Purpose

Selects or temporarily joins several items or nodes at the same time to enable you to perform a command. This method is faster than using Shift-Click for adjacent objects.

### To draw a Marquee Selection box

1. Select the Pick tool (or the Shape tool for nodes) from the Toolbox.

2. Place the cursor on a white space outside the area controlled by the objects to be selected.

3. Drag the mouse until the dashed lines of the Marquee Selection box enclose all the desired objects or nodes.

4. Perform the desired operation immediately.

   Clicking on a blank area cancels the Marquee.

*Notes*

If you are using the Marquee to select arcs or wedges, you must cover an area equal to that of a complete ellipse. You can use the Marquee function with the Shift Key depress, but any currently selected objects will be deselected if they fall inside the box boundaries.

# Node Edit

*Purpose*

A node lies at the end point of every curve segment of a CorelDraw illustration object. The program provides a sophisticated array of operations that enable you to control the nodes and alter the shape of objects. You can use these commands to open and close paths, change the attributes of a segment, or convert lines to and from curves.

*To add, delete, or break nodes*

1. Select the Shape tool from the Toolbox.

2. Double-click on either the node or segment involved. (To add nodes to more than one segment, Shift-Click to select them before double-clicking.)

   The Node Edit selection box appears.

3. Select Add or Delete.

   This operation cannot be used to delete a segment.

### *To close an open path*

1. Select the **Shape** tool from the Toolbox.

2. Shift-Click to select the nodes you want joined or draw a Marquee Selection box around them with the Shape Tool.

3. Double-click on one of the selected nodes.

   The Node Edit Selection box appears.

3. Select **Join**.

   You can perform any fill operations after the path has been closed.

### *To join two separate paths into a single curve*

This operation requires the use of two different commands.

1. Select the **Pick** tool from the Toolbox.

2. Select the two segments involved with the Shift-Click method.

3. From the **Arrange** menu, select **Combine**.

4. Select the **Shape** tool from the Toolbox.

5. Use either the Shift-Click or Marquee Selection method to select the nodes you want to join.

6. Double-click on one of the selected nodes to open the Node Edit menu.

7. Select **Join**.

### *To break a curve and create an open path*

1. Select the **Shape** tool from the Toolbox.

2. Double-click on the node at the place the break is to occur. (To break the object at more than one segment Shift-Click on the nodes.)

3. Double-click on one segment.

   The Node Edit Selection box appears.

3. Select **Break**.

Any fill that was set for the object disappears
when it is broken into an open path.

### *To convert a segment to or from a curve or line*

1. Select the Shape tool from the Toolbox.

2. Double-click on either the node or segment
   involved. (To convert more than one segment,
   Shift-Click to select them before double-clicking.)

   The Node Edit Selection box appears.

3. Select To Line or To Curve.

### *To convert the type of node*

1. Select the Shape tool from the Toolbox.

2. Double-click on either the node or segment
   involved. (To convert more than one segment,
   Shift-Click to select them before double-clicking.)

   The Node Edit Selection box appears.

3. Choose Cusp, Smooth, or Symmet
   (Symmetrical).

### *Note*

For more information on curves, types of nodes, and
control points see the appropriate entry.

# ══ Outline Pen Controls ══

### *Purpose*

Controls the appearance of the boundary of an object.
You can define the type, placement, thickness of lines
and corners, and the angle of the outline pen. You also
can set end caps, such as arrows.

### *To use one of the preset line values*

1. Select the Pick or Shape tool from the Toolbox,
   or go to Step 3 after you draw the object.

2. Click on the object you want to define.

3. Select the Outline tool from the Toolbox.

   The Outline flyout menu appears.

4. Select one of the options to the right of the Pen icon.

   Options include NONE (no visible outline), Hair(line), 1/2 point, 1 point, 2 point, 4 point, and 8 point widths.

### To set custom outline attributes using the Outline Pen dialog box

1. Select the Pick or Shape tool from the Toolbox, or proceed to Step 3 after you draw the object.

2. Click on the object you want to define, or choose a group of objects with the Shift-Click or Marquee Selection method.

3. Select the Outline tool from the Toolbox.

   The Outline flyout menu appears.

4. Select the Pen icon at the upper left of the menu.

   The Outline Pen dialog box appears.

   Choose from the following options:

5. Select the Type of line—None, Solid, Dashed, or Dotted by clicking on the appropriate radio button. (Dashed and Dotted options only work with Postscript printers.)

6. Turn on or off Behind Fill by clicking on the appropriate checkbox.

   This option makes the outline appear half its width. Behind Fill acts as a toggle for the placement of the outline. If the option is turned off, the line is placed in front of the fill. Thicker lines cover part of the fill, and the outline is placed behind and centered on the boundary of the fill.

7. Turn on or off Scale with Image by clicking on the appropriate checkbox.

**Scale With Image** automatically changes the size of the fill line as the object is resized. If the object is reduced, the line shrinks. If it is made larger, the line expands. Calligraphic effects are not affected, no matter how an object is rotated or skewed.

8. Select one of the following **Corner** types:

| | |
|---|---|
| **Miter** | Creates a sharp corner where two lines meet as if the angles were set with a miter saw. The exact angle amount can be set in the Preferences option from the Special menu. |
| **Round** | Gives a soft corner at the spot where two lines meet. Setting this option causes the "pen nib" for the outline to become round. |
| **Bevel** | Squares off the juncture of two lines. |

9. Select from the following settings for **Line Cap**, which is the shape that occurs at the end of a line:

| | |
|---|---|
| **Butt** | Squares off the end of the line with no projections of any sort. |
| **Round** | Produces a perfectly rounded end. |
| **Square** | Gives a flat appearance with a clean 90-degree angle. |
| **Arrowhead** | Creates a proportionally shaped arrowhead at the end of the line. Thin lines produce a small arrowhead. Thicker lines may be more suited as pointers. |

All choices except the arrowhead change both ends of the line. The arrowhead option can be placed at both ends or in combination with any other line cap.

10. Set the thickness of the line by entering a number from the keyboard or clicking the arrows in the Width dialog box.

    You can change the unit of measure by clicking on the current setting to the right of the Width value. Options include inches, centimeters, picas and points, and fractional points.

11. Set any special settings on the angle and shape of the pen (see the *Calligraphic Effects*).

12. Click **OK** to confirm your selections.

### *To set a default Outline for all new objects*

1. Select the **Pick** tool from the Toolbox.

2. Click on a blank area of the page to undo any selected object.

3. Select the **Outline** tool.

4. Click **OK** to set new defaults or **Cancel** to abandon the operation.

5. Set any Outline Tool options.

6. If required, click **OK** in the appropriate dialog boxes.

    You can redefine the defaults at any time.

### *Notes*

The None selection for type of line causes the program to run the fill for the object to the boundary of the outline and draw no outline form.

The 0.00 setting is not the same as NONE. It actually prints a line one pixel high (the same value as Hairline). Use the NONE setting if you want to eliminate printing the outline. On typesetters or high-resolution laser printers a hairline or 0.00 setting may produce a line too thin for most purposes.

To see the appearance of your outline selections, you must enable the Preview window. Dashed and dotted lines do not appear in Preview, but do print on Postscript printers.

One point equals 1/72nd of an inch. The Hairline Rule (line) is traditionally 0.25 point, but actually prints as the smallest line the printer can produce.

Do not set the default line caps to arrows because every open path will then have an arrowhead cap.

See also *Outline Color Controls* and *Calligraphic Effects*.

# Outline Color Controls

## *Purpose*

Sets the shade of gray and color of an object's outline. You can use spot or process colors as well as custom halftone screens (Postscript only) to add definition to your work. Color can be output on a color printer as slides, overhead transparencies, or produced through traditional printing techniques.

## *To use one of the preset line values*

1. Select the **Pick** or **Shape** tool from the Toolbox, or go to Step 3 after you draw the object.

2. Click on the object you want to define.

3. Select the **Outline** tool from the Toolbox.

   The Outline flyout menu appears.

4. Select one of the options to the right of the Brush icon.

   Options include **White**, **Black**, **10**, **20**, **40**, **60**, and **80** percent gray.

## *To set custom outline attributes using the outline brush options*

1. Select the **Pick** or **Shape** tool from the Toolbox, or go to Step 3 after you draw the object.

2. Click on the object you want to define, or choose a group of objects with the Shift-Click or Marquee Selection method.

3. Select the Outline tool from the Toolbox.

4. Click on the Brush icon at the lower left of the flyout bar.

   The Outline Color dialog box appears.

5. Select Spot or Process color.

   If you select Spot color, set the following options:

   Color            Enter a numeric value or
                    click on the arrows to the
                    right of the entry area.

   Tint             Enter a numeric value or
                    click on the arrows to the
                    right of the entry area. The
                    PANTONE color number
                    appears below the color
                    display window.

   If you select Process color, set the desired color by combining the Cyan, Magenta, Yellow, and Black values in the entry boxes. Enter numbers or click on the arrows to the right of the entry area. The current color appears in the display window.

6. If you have a Postscript printer and you choose Spot color, you also can select Halftone Screen settings. (See *Halftones*.)

7. Click OK to confirm your choices or Cancel to abandon the operation.

## *To set a default outline color for all new objects*

   1. Select the Pick tool from the Toolbox.

   2. Click on a blank area of the page to undo any selected object.

   3. Select the Outline tool.

   4. You are asked if you want to set new defaults. Click OK to proceed or Cancel to abandon the

operation.

5. Set any Outline options you want to use.

6. Click OK as required in the appropriate dialog boxes.

   All new objects are created with the defaults you just set. You can redefine the defaults at any time.

*Note*

PANTONE colors seen on the screen may not match the actual color. Refer to a PANTONE Color Reference Manual, available at art supply stores or from your printer, for choosing the proper shade. See also *Spot or Process Color*.

# Page Setup

*Purpose*

Sets the orientation and size of the page that is displayed on-screen. You can choose one of six predefined sizes or set custom values. Combining Page Setup with the Print Crop Marks and Crosshairs options from the Print menu can make it easier to send a nonstandard page to your print shop.

*To set the page orientation and size*

1. With any tool, select the Files menu.

2. Select Page Setup.

3. Select Portrait (vertical) or Landscape (horizontal) orientation.

4. Select from the following page sizes: Letter, Legal, Tabloid, A3, A4, A5, B5, or Custom.

5. If you select Custom, set the actual page dimensions in the two entry boxes by entering a

value or clicking on the arrows in the appropriate boxes marked **Horizontal** and **Vertical**.

6. Click **OK** to confirm the settings or **Cancel** to abandon the operation.

*Notes*

The Page Setting does not actually change the Windows/Corel Printer setup. You must install your output device via the Windows Setup program or Control Panel. Some Postscript printers may not require adjustment for print orientation.

The A3 through B5 settings are common European paper sizes.

You can toggle the unit of measure in the Horizontal and Vertical entry boxes by clicking on the word. Choices include inches, centimeters, pica and points, and fractional points.

# PANTONE Colors

*Purpose*

Produces exact colors through the use of the PANTONE Color Matching System and the Spot color options. This method identifies colors by number. A printer uses the number to accurately choose an ink to reproduce the color.

*To create master separations for spot color printing on a Postscript printer*

1. Use the PANTONE Color Guide as a reference for choosing colors.

2. Keep the number of colors to a minimum. If many different colors are used, it may be less expensive to use process color.

3. When the drawing is complete, save your work by doing the following:

- From the Files menu, select Save.

- Enter a name for the illustration and click OK.

4. From the File menu, select Print.

5. Select Print As Separations.

6. Click OK.

7. Select All Colors or Selected Colors by clicking on the appropriate radio button.

| | |
|---|---|
| All Colors | Prints a separate page for each color. |
| Selected Colors | Prints a page for each color you choose from the selection box to the left. Use the Shift-Click method to select more than one color. Clicking again on a color deselects it. |

8. Click OK to confirm your choices.

### Notes

If you plan to send work to an outside printer, limit all color settings to spot color, rather than a mix of spot and process.

Variables in monitors, monitor settings, and color cards may cause PANTONE colors to appear different than the colors printed in the PANTONE Reference Guide. Choose colors based on the printed samples, and give that number to the printer.

# Place Duplicate

### Purpose

Makes an exact copy of an object placed a specific distance from the original. Use this feature to create drop shadow effects and place boxes and lines in forms. This command differs from the Cut or Copy

commands because no object is placed in the
Clipboard.

## *To add a copy of an object using the place duplicate command*

1. Select the **Pick** tool from the Toolbox.

2. Select the object you want to duplicate.

3. Press **Ctrl-D**.

4. To place additional copies of the same object, keep pressing **D**.

   Release the Control key after you place all duplicates.

## *To set the amount of off-set for objects created using place duplicate*

1. Use any tool to open the **Special** menu.

2. Select **Preferences**.

3. To change the unit of measure for the Place Duplicate option, click on the current selection. Options include inches, centimeters, picas and points, and fractional points.

4. Set the amount of **Horizontal** offset in the left-most box marked Place Duplicate. (The direction of movement is not labeled.)

5. Set the amount of **Vertical** offset in the right-most box marked Place Duplicate. (The direction of movement is not labeled.)

   Settings with positive numbers place the new object up toward the right of the original, and negative numbers set the new object down to the left.

## *Notes*

The new object you create automatically is selected.

You can use the Marquee Selection, Group, or Combine commands to duplicate several objects at once. Use Combine only if you want the objects combined into one.

# Polygons

## Purpose

Creates a multisegment set of curves or lines. The final object may have an open or closed path.

## To create a multisegment set of curves

1. Select the Freehand tool from the Toolbox.

2. Draw the first segment by doing the following:

   Click and drag the mouse to form a curve.

   or

   Click, move and click the mouse again to draw a straight line.

   or

   Click, move and click the mouse again as you press the Constrain key to draw a straight line, which is exactly horizontal, vertical, or an angle that is in an increment of 15 degrees.

3. Double-click or click and drag the mouse from the end point of the curve or line you just created.

4. Repeat Step 3 until all segments are created.

5. To create the last segment, click the mouse once (for a straight line), or release the mouse button (for a curve) at the end point. To form a closed path, you must place the cursor above the start of the object.

## To create an octagon

1. Select the Ellipse tool.

2. Draw a circle the diameter of the desired octagon by pressing and holding the Constrain (Control) key as you drag the mouse.

3. Press the space bar to get the Pick tool.

4. From the Arrange menu, select Convert To Curves.

5. Select the **Shape** tool from the Toolbox.

6. Draw a Marquee Selection box around the circle.

7. Double-click on one of the nodes.

8. From the Node Edit pop-up menu, select **Add**.

9. Double-click the mouse once again on a node.

10. Select **To Line**.

### *To create a diamond*

1. Select the **Ellipse** tool.

2. Draw a circle the diameter of the desired octagon by pressing and holding the **Constrain** (Control) key as you drag the mouse.

3. Press the **space bar** to get the Pick tool.

4. From the **Arrange** menu, select **Convert To Curves**.

5. Select the **Shape** tool from the Toolbox.

6. Draw a Marquee Selection box around the circle.

7. Double-click the mouse on one of the nodes.

8. From the Node Edit pop-up menu, select **To Line**.

### *Notes*

As you draw a straight line with the **Constrain** key, the Status Line indicates the length and angle of the line both in absolute size and relative to the page.

If you created a closed path, the right-hand side of the Status Line displays **Fill** and any current fill pattern or color.

# Postscript Textures

### *Purpose*

Fills an object with complex patterns that can be sent to a postscript printer. You can fill an object with a brick wall, stars, bubbles, cracks, fish scales, and even text characters. CorelDraw provides a basic set of 42 patterns, but by adjusting the various parameters you can radically alter the appearance of a given fill. Due to the number of variables, this book outlines the basic steps used to create a Postscript Textured Fill. Examples of the different basic styles are available in Appendix A of the CorelDraw Users' Guide.

### To fill an object with Postscript textures

1. Create an object that can be filled by using any of the CorelDraw tools.

2. Select the object.

   You can fill more than one object at a time by using the Shift-Click method or the Marquee Select method.

3. Select the **Fill** tool from the Toolbox.

4. Select the **Postscript** icon, which is marked with the letters PS.

5. Refer to the illustrations in Appendix A of the CorelDraw Users' Guide to see examples of the available textures and sample settings.

6. Click on the name of the desired texture. Click on the arrows to see additional listings.

   The five number entry boxes below the selection box enable you to set parameters. Based on the texture you select, four or five options are presented. If a box is not in use, it is labeled *** UNUSED *** and has a default of zero.

7. Change any of the values you want by entering a specific number or clicking on the arrows next to the box.

9. Click **OK** to accept the settings or **Cancel** to abandon the operation.

   The Status Line shows the Postscript Texture name of the currently selected object.

   Note that the actual pattern of the fill cannot be seen in the Preview window. A pattern containing the letters PS appears.

The following list contains the common parameters of the Postscript Texture dialog box:

### Frequency

Sets the number of times the complete pattern repeats per inch. Larger numbers make the fill pattern smaller.

### LineWidth

Measures the width of the line in 1/1000th of an inch. In some cases, the design has more than one line, and settings appear for LineWidth1, LineWidth2, etc.

### GrayN, BackgroundGray, ForegroundGray

Sets the shade of gray for the section or part of the fill indicated in the name. The higher the number you set, the darker the shade. Zero is white and 100 is black. In many cases setting the BackgroundGray or Gray to a negative number makes the fill transparent. Gray3 is opaque at any value.

### Number

Determines the number of objects in a given figure, such as spokes in a complete circle (360 degrees). NumberSqInch is the number of repetitions in a square inch.

### Points

Sets number of points in star shapes. For example, to get a five pointed star, use setting 5.

### Random Seed

Modifies the random pattern in some objects. Changing the object's size in any way alters the generation, so make sure that you size and scale the object before setting and testing this value.

### Spacing

Places the pattern elements relative to a percent of the default unit of measure. Lower numbers place the pattern elements closer, and larger settings space the elements farther apart.

### MaxSize, MinSize, MaxGray, MinGray

Some textures have a random variation in size or shade of the elements of the pattern. Max* sets the upper limit, and Min* sets the lower limit.

## Tips

Draw a simple shape such as a rectangle or an ellipse to test your Postscript Texture's appearance. Use an ellipse if your final output will have many curved elements. This test run cuts the printing time required by showing how the settings will look.

No hard and fast rules exist for using the Postscript Textures feature, and the lack of Preview and possible printer delays discourage some people. Try using some of the simple patterns first.

## Notes

The use of Postscript Textures is limited to Postscript-compatible printers or output devices. Print times vary greatly depending on the settings you select. Some Postscript emulations and early versions of Postscript printers cannot handle the complexity of these fills, and you may have difficulty with very complex patterns on any device. If you have trouble with a given texture, try using one of the settings given in Appendix A of the Users' Guide for that texture. Also try removing any outline fills.

Printing only the textured object may speed printing. Use the **Print Only Selected** option in the Printer Options. If you are exporting the drawing with textures to a desktop publishing program, you may have to remove everything else from the page to print.

A list of font numbers for setting values for the Text Texture is shown on page 22 of Appendix A in the CorelDraw Users' Guide. The characters are entered using the ASCII code number. Do not use the leading zero. For example, a setting of Font=30 and Character=67 fills the object with repetitions of the letter C in the Palatino typeface.

# Preview

### Purpose

Enables you to see the effect of commands on an object, and to see how it will look after printing. To speed up program operation, CorelDraw displays only the outlines or *wireframes* of an object in the working area. You cannot see the thickness of lines, end caps, fills, and other attributes you select for that element.

### To enable or disable the Preview window

1. With any tool, open the Display menu.

2. Select Show Preview.

   The Preview window opens if closed and disappears if currently selected.

### Keyboard Shortcut

Press F3.

### To size the Preview window

1. With the Pick, Shape, Text, or a drawing tool active, place the cursor on the inner top or bottom border of the Preview window.

2. Drag the mouse to enlarge or reduce the size of the Preview window.

3. Release the mouse button after the window is the size you want. Both the Preview and working windows adjust to the new dimensions.

   Dragging the Preview window to less than half its normal height or width shifts its position to or from the right or lower portion of the screen. Use this size when you work with illustrations that are wide and short, or tall and thin.

### To preview only the selected object

1. With any tool selected, open the Display menu.

2. Select Preview Selected Only.

If you are interested in observing effects on objects positioned behind other objects, select Preview Selected Only. Using this feature speeds up screen redraw for complex drawings.

### To toggle the Auto-Update feature

1. With any tool selected, open the Display menu.

2. Select Auto-Update.

   Repeat the operation to reverse the selection.

   If Auto-Update is enabled, the Preview window automatically redraws to show any changes made to the working area. If Preview is inactive, you must click with the mouse inside the window to update its information.

### Notes

The following Postscript features do not appear in the Preview window as they will look after printing:

• Any dashed or dotted lines appear as solid lines. You can confirm that a line is dotted or dashed by selecting the object and checking the setting in the Outline Pen dialog box.

• Grayscale and rotated bitmap images that are imported into CorelDraw do not display grayscale tones.

• Postscript halftone screen settings do not appear in the Preview window. Confirm the settings by selecting the object and reviewing the appropriate dialog box.

• Postscript Textures cannot be viewed in the Preview window, but when the object is selected the Status Line does show the name of the texture behind the word Fill on the right-hand side of the screen.

• Any bitmap that was imported with the For Tracing option will not print at all.

Any use of the mouse to invoke a command interrupts the redrawing of the Preview window. Some complex actions, such as radial fills, may take a few seconds to stop drawing in the Preview window.

# Preview Toolbox

### Purpose

Enables you to control the operation of the update mode, and orientation and magnification of the Preview window. The Preview window is controlled by the Preview Toolbox Zoom tool. When the Preview Toolbox is closed (hidden), the Preview Window operates normally depending on the options selected in the Display menu.

### To open or close the Preview window toolbox

1. Use any tool to open the Display menu.

2. Click on the Show Preview Toolbox.

### Keyboard Shortcut

Alt-D-T

### To change the area displayed in the Preview window with the Preview Zoom tool

1. Use any tool to select the Zoom icon in the Preview Toolbox. The icon resembles a magnifying glass.

2. Select one of the following options:

| | |
|---|---|
| Zoom In | Zooms in on any area of a drawing you select. The icon resembles a magnifying glass with a plus sign. When the mouse button is released, the zoomed area fills the Preview area. |
| Zoom Out | Reverts the Preview to either a view equal to the one before the last use of Zoom, or doubles the area to twice that at the time (if possible). |

| | |
|---|---|
| | The icon resembles a magnifying glass with a minus sign. |
| **1:1** | Changes the view to approximately a one-to-one ratio with the printer output (one inch equals one inch). The exact ratio varies depending on the type of monitor and the Windows screen driver in use. |
| **All** | Places every object in the drawing (on or off the page) inside the Preview window. |
| **Show Page** | Shifts the Preview window to include the entire print area. The icon appears as a shadowed rectangle. |

### *To change the view in the Preview window using the scroll bars*

1. The Preview Toolbox must be active.

2. Use the mouse with any tool to drag the button on the vertical or horizontal scroll bar, or click on the arrows in the scroll bar corners.

3. Release the button.

   The image visible in the Preview window moves in relation to the shift in the button on the bar without changing magnification.

### *To change To/From Vertical or Horizontal Windows*

1. The Preview Toolbox must be active.

2. With the mouse, select one of the icons under the Preview Toolbox Zoom icon.

   - The upper icon shows two tall windows side by side. Click on this icon to obtain a pair of vertical windows with the Preview window to the right of the working area if the current mode is horizontal.

- The lower icon shows a pair of windows stacked one above the other. Use this icon to place the Preview window below the work area.

## Notes

When the Preview Toolbox is shown, the Preview window view moves independently of the working area.

# Printing

## Purpose

Provides you with a means to produce hard copy in a variety of formats in both black and white and color. You can send output to any printer that has a Windows driver, as well as writing the file to disk to send to services such as typesetting. The exact features available depend on the printer and drawing involved.

Before performing any print command from CorelDraw, you must properly install your output device via the Windows Setup Program or Control Panel. For more information on this topic, refer to your Windows User Guide. You also must have the proper printer chosen as the active printer via the Windows Control Panel.

## To send a drawing directly to the printer

1. Use any tool to open the File menu.

2. Select Print.

   Some of the options in this dialog box are dependent on the printer you use and may not be available.

3. Select the options you want to use.

   Most printers support the following options:

### Print Only Selected

Limits the output to objects that were selected in the drawing at the time the Print menu was opened. Choose this feature to test portions of a complex drawing, such as those with Postscript textures or complicated fills.

### Scale

Enters a number equal to the percent of magnification or reduction desired. You can shrink or expand the output. The default is 100 percent. For example, a setting of 50 percent gives a half size image. If you are printing larger than the available paper size, you also must choose the Title option. This option has no effect on the actual Corel drawing, only the printed output.

### Tile

Prints portions that are outside the boundaries of your page format, and also prints objects at a larger magnification than that which can fit on a single page. The output is done on as many pages as required, rather than on a single page.

### Fit To Page

Alters the size of the output image. Objects sent to the printer fill the entire page. Sizes of objects within the drawing are not altered.

### Print To File

Causes the output to be written to a file on disk, rather than sent to the printer. Use this selection to save the work for later printing, or to provide a usable file to a typesetter that does not have CorelDraw installed on a computer. You are prompted for a file name, which usually bears a .PRN extension. If the person who will later output the file requires a different extension, you can change the extension when naming the file. If you are sending the file to a different type of device than the one installed for Windows, install the matching driver and select it using the Windows Control Panel.

The following options only work with a Postscript printer connected and properly installed, or if you are having it printed by a Postscript device (such as a Linotronic 330 composition system).

### Include File Info (Postscript only)

Prints the file name, color model and color (including number for PANTONE selections), screen resolution and angle, and the date and time on the side of the page. The Page Setup must show smaller page dimensions than the actual size of the paper used by the printer. Use at least a one-inch smaller setting so that CorelDraw has space to place the file information.

### Crop marks and Crosshairs

Produces masters for printing color separations, or crop marks for use as cutting or paste-up guides. Crosshairs (more commonly known as registration marks) are used to precisely line up images on color separations. CorelDraw places crop marks and registration marks in the corners of the page, as well as a gradient scale for use by your print shop. The Page Setup must show smaller page dimensions than the actual size of the paper used by the printer. Use a one-inch smaller setting so that CorelDraw has space to place the file information.

### Print As Separations

Prints a separate page for each color and fill setting. If you choose Spot, a page for each individual color prints. Process color elements cause four pages to be generated. Don't mix spot and color options in the same drawing.

### Film Negative

Converts the file to a mirror image and reverses all black and white values giving the same appearance as a photographic negative.

### All Fonts Resident

Limits fonts to resident Postscript fonts, or ones that have been downloaded. Selecting this feature results in the printer fonts being used instead of the CorelDraw set. The output looks better than the Corel fonts, especially at small point sizes. Any fonts you do not have print in Courier.

### Custom Screen Frequency

Sets the screen frequency for various resolutions. Corel's normal default is 60 dpi, which is the right setting for a 300 dpi printer. If you are sending work to a high quality Postscript device, adjust the setting based on the resolution of the typesetter. Use the default value for halftones in the drawing as you design outlines and fills.

4. Click OK to confirm your choices and start the print job, or Cancel to abandon the operation.

### To choose or check the default printer or setting a new timeout value

1. Use any tool to open the File menu.

2. Select Control Panel.

3. Select the Printers icon.

4. Double-click on the name of the printer you want to use in the Installed Printers selection box.

5. Make sure that printer is shown as the active printer in the Status box. Click on the active radio button if it is not.

6. Click on the Configure command button.

7. Make sure that the correct port (such as LPT1) is highlighted, and that the name of the selected printer shows at the top of the Printers-Configure dialog box.

8. Check settings if you are using a serial printer such as an AppleLaser Writer.

9. Set the Transmission Retry value from 600 to 999 seconds. Drag the mouse to highlight the current number, press Del, and type the new value.

10. Click OK to confirm your choices.

11. Click OK to exit the Printers dialog box.

12. Close the Control Panel and return to CorelDraw.

(The Control Panel is a Microsoft Windows application. For more information refer to Chapter 5 of the Window's Users Guide.) Use your printer documentation to decide how exact settings should be made.

The preceding instructions are for Windows 3.0.
Prior Windows versions may have different setup
routines.

## Tips

If you send a drawing to the printer and get a blank
page or part of the drawing is missing, check the
setting for outlines and fills. If the setting is NONE or
White, you are printing with invisible ink.

You can create registration marks without using the
Crop Marks and Crosshairs option by drawing your
own with the colors being used.

## Notes

Printing problems are the most common reason for
technical support calls in the computer industry.
Although the Windows interface provides the basic
output services for CorelDraw, it does place another
layer of complexity in the process. Before assuming
something is wrong, make sure that all the settings
match your hardware, and that all the components are
properly installed and connected. The phone bill you
save could be your own. You can speed up operation
of the printer by disabling the Windows Print Spooler
or Print Manager.

If you are using a Postscript printer driver from
Micrograpfx, make sure that the [CorelDrivers] section
in your WIN.INI file has the line MGXPS=1 listed. You
can edit the file using the Windows Notepad or any
editor that saves a file in plain ASCII text. Be careful.
Windows may not operate properly, or applications
such as Corel may not load if you do not edit the
WIN.INI file correctly. Make a backup of the file—just
in case.

If you are using a Postscript printer and are having
trouble printing bitmap images inside a CorelDraw file,
make sure that your printer is set to the Postscript
Batch Mode.

If your printer acts as if it is printing yet nothing prints,
check the Timeout setting.

HP Laserjets should have *at least* 1.5 megabytes of memory for use with graphics applications. Less than that amount of memory results in complex drawings being printed in pieces on several pages.

Memory, speed, type of interface, laser engine, toner cartridges, and overall design effect how fast a given job prints on two different machines.

# Process Color

### *Purpose*

Uses a combination of the primary colors cyan, magenta, and yellow, combined with black to produce virtually any shade and hue. If you want to use a large number of colors, process color generally saves money compared to spot color. You cannot see colors in the working area. Use the Preview window to see how the process color looks.

You can print process colors directly to a color printer without separations, such as the HP Paintjet or QMS Colorscript using the File menu. You can print the drawing as separations to be reproduced by a commercial printer.

### *To select process colors*

1. Create an object using any combination of CorelDraw tools or commands. Closed Path objects can be filled, and all objects can contain custom outlines.

2. Select the appropriate dialog box for the fill or outline you want.

3. Set any noncolor options for the operation.

4. Select Process Color.

5. Set the values for the four process colors.

   100 is the highest for any single entry box.

6. If you are using linear or radial fountain fills, you must designate settings for the From and To

boxes. From sets the beginning shade and it is blended towards the To setting.

An approximation of the color combination appears in a window to the left of the entry boxes.

7. Click **OK** to confirm your color choice.

8. Click **OK** to exit any higher level dialog boxes.

### *To print process colors using the color separation method*

1. Use any tool to open the **File** menu.

2. Select **Print**.

   The Print Options dialog box appears. Make sure that you have a Postscript device selected as the active printer; process separations do not work on any other type of printer.

3. Place an X in the checkbox for Crop marks and Crosshairs.

4. Select **Print As Separations**.

5. Select any other options you want.

6. Click **OK**.

7. From the Color Separations dialog box, select **All Colors**.

8. Click **OK**.

9. Click **OK** to confirm your choices and start the print job, or **Cancel** to abandon the operation.

   Only the colors you actually use to make up the combinations print. For example, if you do not use yellow in any operation, no page prints for yellow.

### *Notes*

Due to differences in hardware configurations and display settings, it is impossible to be sure that the process color shown in the display window will match the final output. If you must have an exact color and do not have too many colors in a drawing, consider using spot color.

The Postscript Halftone Screen option does not work with process color. If you must have a halftone screen for a given effect, you must use the Spot color option.

Setting a process color value for outlines or fills with no object selected causes that setting to be used as a default for new objects. This value selection can save a lot of time if you are using one process color for several objects. You can redefine the default at any time. Specific elements can be given individual outlines or fills at any time.

As a rule, do not mix process and spot color models in the same illustration.

You must have a Postscript printer driver installed and selected to print color separations using CorelDraw. You can use the Print option to write a file to disk that can be printed by a service bureau, without a Postscript printer actually attached to your system. See *Print*.

# Quit

### *Purpose*

Provides a proper exit from the program.

### *To exit CorelDraw*

1. Use any tool to select the File menu.

2. Select Quit.

   If you saved your work, the program terminates. If you have not saved your work, continue with the steps in this listing.

   You are prompted to save your work.

3. Choose Yes to save your work, or No to terminate the program. Selecting Cancel returns you to CorelDraw.

   If you choose Yes, a File Selection box appears.

4. Enter a name for the file.

5. Click **OK**.

CorelDraw will be terminated.

### Keyboard Shortcut
**Ctrl-Q**

# Rectangles and Squares

### Purpose
Creates rectangles and squares with the use of the Rectangle tool from the Toolbox. The objects can be converted into curved elements.

### To create a rectangle
1. Select the **Rectangle** tool from the Toolbox (the square-shaped icon).

   The cursor becomes a thin cross shape.

2. Place the mouse cursor at the start point.

3. Drag the mouse at an angle to the end point.

4. Release the mouse button.

   Pressing the Shift key as you draw a rectangle causes the rectangle to appear at the point at which you began dragging the mouse.

### To create a perfect square
1. Select the **Rectangle** tool from the Toolbox (the square-shaped icon).

   The cursor becomes a thin cross shape.

2. Place the mouse cursor at the start point.

3. Press the **Constrain** (Control) key.

3. Drag the mouse at an angle to the end point.

4. Release the mouse button.

5. Release the Constrain key.

Pressing the Shift key as you draw a square causes the square to appear at the point at which you began dragging the mouse.

### To change a rectangle or square to a curved object

1. Select the **Pick** tool from the Toolbox.

2. Click on the target object.

3. From the **Arrange** menu, select **Convert To Curves**.

4. Make any changes to the shape of the object with the Shape tool and Node Edit commands.

### To round corners on rectangles or squares

1. Select the **Shape** tool from the Toolbox.

2. Select the target object.

3. Drag any one of the nodes at the corners along the side of the object.

   As you move the node, the corners become more and more rounded. You can turn a square into a circle. (This technique does not have the same node configuration as a circle created with the Ellipse tool.)

### Tip

If you need to make rectangles or squares of an exact size, set the Grid to a comfortable unit that divides evenly into the desired size (such as .25 inches for half inch objects). For more information see *Grid*.

Use of the Align, Repeat, and Place Duplicate commands can speed design forms and similar tasks.

### Note

The Status Line shows the height and width of the object as it is being drawn, and the word `Rectangle` appears after the process is completed.

# Repeat

### Purpose

Applies the most recently executed command to the currently selected object.

### To repeat a command

1. Perform the original operation.

2. Select the Pick or Shape tool.

3. Click on the object.

4. From the Edit menu, select Repeat.

### Keyboard Shortcut

Ctrl-R

### Note

You can continue to press Ctrl-R to create a series of objects.

# Rotate and Skew Objects

### Purpose

Rotates or skews an object or group of objects to any angle. Use this command to slant or turn an object. You can also change the center of rotation.

### To rotate an object using the mouse

1. Select the Pick tool from the Toolbox.

2. Double-click on the object.

   Arrows replace the selection handles, and a circle with a dot appears in the middle of the object.

3. If you want to rotate the object around a specific point, drag the COR to that position with the mouse.

4. Place the cursor, which changes to a maltese cross shape, over one of the arrows and drag in the desired direction.

Dragging one of the four curved corner arrow sets rotates the object. Dragging any of the four straight arrow sets skews the object.

5. Release the mouse button after the object shifts the way you want.

### To rotate an object using the menu method

1. Select the Pick tool from the Toolbox.

2. Open the Rotate and Skew option.

The Rotate and Skew dialog box appears.

3. Set either the angle of rotation, or the degree of horizontal or vertical skewing by typing numbers from the keyboard or clicking on the arrows. A compass rose is displayed to aid in choosing values.

4. Click OK.

5. Repeat Steps 3 and 4 as desired.

### Keyboard Shortcut

Alt-T-R

The Status Line displays the exact angle of rotation or skewing for the current operation as you move the object with the mouse. Note that this figure is not the total of all movements, but the value for the current operation.

### Notes

If you want to rotate and skew by using the menu method, you must open the menu twice.

If you want to use the menu method to rotate an object around a new center of rotation, you must reposition the center marker before you open the menu.

You can toggle between Rotate and Skew or Stretch and Scale modes by clicking on the object with the mouse.

You can modify bitmap images with these commands like any other object, but remember that you must print these images on a Postscript device. Crop or perform any other functions first. A rotated or skewed bitmap appears as a featureless gray shape, with a white triangle to indicate the orientation.

# Rulers

### *Purpose*

Provides a set of optional rulers that you use to measure distance and size in the working area.

### *To show or hide rulers*

1. With any tool, open the Display menu.

2. Select Show Rulers.

   Repeating the operation reverses the selection. An arrow to the left of the selection indicates the rulers are visible.

### *Note*

The unit of measure is determined by the current unit of measure for the grid. For more information on setting the Grid see that listing.

# Save/Save As

### *Purpose*

Provides a means of saving work to disk. Use Save to create a new file name or update an existing file. Use the Save As command to save your work under a new name without disturbing the existing file. This command enables you to have two or more versions of a drawing.

### *To save your work*

1. With any tool selected, open the File menu.

2. Choose either Save or Save As.

   If the file name exists, the existing version is overwritten and you immediately return to the program. If you want to keep the original versions intact, do the following additional steps:

3. Enter a name for the file from the File Selection menu.

4. Click OK to save the current work under the chosen name.

### *Note*

If you previously saved the drawing, the path and file name appear in the File Selection box.

# Select All/Select Next

### *Purpose*

Provides a quick method for choosing all the objects in a drawing, or selecting objects hidden under other objects.

### *To select all objects in a drawing*

1. Select the Pick tool from the Edit menu.

2. Select Select All.

3. Perform any available series of commands.

### *Keyboard Shortcut*

Alt-E-S

### *To select an object with the Select Next feature*

1. Select the Pick tool from the Toolbox.

2. Press the Tab key to select an object.

3. Continue pressing Tab until the desired object is selected.

## Notes

If you use the Select Next command, the Status Line displays the type of object and its current fill. If you use the Select All command, the Status Line displays the number of objects.

The objects selected with these commands operate as if you selected them with the Pick tool or the Marquee Selection methods.

# Setting Preferences

## Purpose

Enables you to customize the operation of the Freehand tool and certain commands to suit your needs. For more information on the operation of a given CorelDraw function see the appropriate listing in this Quick Reference.

## To customize CorelDraw

1. With any tool, open the Special menu.

2. Select Preferences.

   The Preferences dialog box appears. The dialog box is divided into these sections: Lines and Curves, Print/Preview, and Miscellaneous.

3. Change the values of any of the options by entering the desired number or letter, or by clicking the arrows to the right of the entry box.

   Lines and Curves affects the way the Freehand tool places and interprets how curve and line segments are formed. Values for the options under the Lines and Curves Section are measured in pixels, ranging from one to 10. The options in this section include the following:

**Freehand Tracking**

Causes the Freehand tool to follow minor movements at a lower setting. Results in a smoother looking line at higher settings.

**Autotrace Tracking**

Works the same as Freehand Tracking, but changes the way the Corel Auto-Trace pen follows a line or curve.

**Corner Threshold**

Works with any curve or line with Freehand drawing or the Auto-Trace command (other than a straight line drawn with the click method). Lower numbers predispose the program to create cusps and sharper breaks at corners, higher settings result in more segments defined as straight lines.

**Straight Line Threshold**

Yields more curves when the program interprets a segment at a lower setting. Higher numbers result in more lines.

**Autojoin**

Sets the maximum number of pixels between the ends of lines or curves when objects are joined.

**Print/Preview** controls how mitered corners and fountain fills display and print. The following options are available:

**Miter Limit**

Sets the lower limit (in degrees) for mitering corners. Any corners meeting at less than this angle are beveled automatically.

| Fountain Stripes | Determines the number of steps that are used to create radial and linear fills in both the Preview window and on non-Postscript printers. Adjusting this number may produce smoother looking fills. |

Miscellaneous options include the following:

| Place Duplicate | Determines the offset used to position a new object created with the Place Duplicate command relative to the original object. |
| Typeface Selection Character | Enables you to change the characters that appears in the display window when you have the Text dialog box open. Type the desired character. If the character you select is not available in the typeface you are using, the letter A is displayed. |

*Note*

You can change the unit of measure for the Place Duplicate entry by clicking on the current setting. Options include inches, centimeters, pica and point, and fractional points.

# Show Bitmaps

*Purpose*

Turns on or off the display of bitmaps in the working area. When Show Bitmaps is turned off, the area they occupy is displayed as a hollow rectangle or square. This setting can speed up the redrawing of the screen, and does not have any effect on the Preview window display of bitmap images or the actual printing.

### *To toggle the display of bitmaps in the working area*
1. With any tool, open the Display menu.

2. Select Show Bitmaps.

   Repeating the procedure toggles the feature on and off.

### *Keyboard Shortcut*
Alt-D-B

### *Note*
Although this feature works with bitmaps imported for tracing, it is not very useful because you cannot see the portions of the bitmap you want to trace.

# Spacing/Straighten Text

### *Purpose*
Modifies the appearance of text by moving characters, adjusting the space between individual characters (kerning), between words, and the amount of space between lines.

### *To set text string spacing with the Text Spacing dialog box*
1. Select the existing text with the Pick tool and press Ctrl-T.

   or

   If you are entering a new string of text, select the Text tool from the toolbox and click the cursor over the desired location.

2. Make any desired changes in the main Text tool dialog box.

3. Click on the Spacing command button.

4. Enter the values for interword, intercharacter, or interline spacing as desired.

   Interword and character spacing are measured in ems. Positive numbers increase spacing and negative numbers decrease the space. Intercharacter and interword spacing is equal to the height of a capital M in the point size of the font in use. Interline spacing is a percent of the point size.

***To adjust kerning or interword spacing interactively with the Shape tool***

1. Select the Shape tool from the Toolbox.

2. Click on the text.

3. Place the cursor over the gray arrow at the right end of the string.

4. To adjust kerning, drag the mouse to the right to increase the spacing or left to decrease the interval of space.

5. Press and hold the Constrain key and drag the mouse to the right to increase or left to decrease the interval or interword spacing.

***To interactively move individual characters with the Shape tool***

1. Select the Shape tool from the Toolbox.

2. Click on the text string that contains the character or characters you want to move.

3. Select an individual character by clicking on its node (the one to its left), or a group of characters using the Shift-click or Marquee Selection method.

4. Drag the node or nodes in the desired direction. A dotted outline of the letters shows the position as you move the mouse.

5. Release the mouse button when you reach the new position.

Holding the Constrain key during the dragging operation limits movement to the nearest baseline, even if is rotated.

### Notes

You also can convert text objects to curves and use other CorelDraw commands such as Rotate, Skew, Size, Scale, and Mirror on text objects.

See also *Edit Text*.

# Spot/PANTONE Color

### Purpose

Enables you to use color as part of a drawing. Exact colors can be printed as part of an illustration produced in CorelDraw through use of the PANTONE Color Matching System and the Spot color options. PANTONE is a method of identifying colors by number. A printer can use that number to accurately choose an ink to reproduce your color. You must provide a separate page with each individual PANTONE color to your printer. Color separations can be printed only on a Postscript printer. If you are using a color output device such as an HP Paintjet or a slide maker, the PANTONE color set can help make the job of choosing colors easier, even if you may not get exactly the same value.

### To select colors when outlining or filling objects

1. Use the PANTONE Color Guide as a reference for choosing colors if you require an exact color.

2. Keep the number of colors to a minimum.

   If many different colors are used it may be less expensive to use Process color.

3. Create the object using any combination of CorelDraw tools.

4. Select Spot color to use color in an outline or fill.

5. Set the number for the color you desire, or click the arrows next to the entry box to change the setting.

6. Linear and radial fountain fills require that you enter a value in the `From` and `To` boxes. `From` sets the beginning shade, and that shade is blended toward the `To` setting.

   An approximation of the color combination is displayed in a window to the left of the entry boxes.

7. When the color is as desired, click `OK` to confirm your choice.

8. Click `OK` to exit any higher level dialog boxes.

---

*To print spot colors using the color separation method (actual color will be produced by a print shop using a different ink for each color)*

1. Use any tool to open the `File` menu.

2. Select `Print`.

   The Print Options dialog box appears. Make sure that you select a Postscript device as the active printer. Color separations do not print on any other type of printer.

3. Place an X in the checkbox for `Crop marks and Crosshairs` by clicking with the mouse.

4. Select `Print As Separations`.

5. Choose any other desired options.

6. Click `OK`.

7. Select `All Colors` or the colors you want to print .

8. Click `OK`.

9. Click `OK` to confirm your choices and start the print job or `Cancel` to abandon the operation.

   A separate page prints for each color selected.

*Notes*

If you have a printer installed with a proper Windows driver, such as an HP Paintjet, you can print directly without using the color separation method.

The Tint value simply makes the color whiter (lower setting) or darker (higher setting). Only one page prints for any given PANTONE color, no matter how many Tint values for that color you set for different objects in the drawing.

Setting a spot color value for outlines or fills with no object selected causes that setting to be used as a default for new objects, which can save time if you are using a color for several objects. You can redefine the default at any time. Specific elements can be given individual outlines or fills.

As a rule, do not mix process and spot color models in the same illustration.

Because variables in monitors, monitor settings, and color cards can distort the displayed PANTONE colors, choose PANTONE colors based on the printed samples, and give that number to your printer.

You must have a Postscript printer driver installed and selected to print color separations using CorelDraw. You can use the Print option to write a file to disk and then have the file printed by a service bureau. See the *Print* listing in this book for more information.

# Starting CorelDraw

*Purpose*

Loads the CorelDraw program. The Open and New commands enable you to retrieve an existing drawing or begin a new drawing.

### *To load CorelDraw*

1. Load Microsoft Windows.

2. Double-click on the CorelDraw icon.

   or

   Double-click on the CORELDRW.EXE file in the File Manager.

   The program appears on-screen.

### *To begin a new drawing*

1. With any tool, open the File menu.

2. Select New.

   If you have work on-screen that you have not saved, you are prompted to save the file, cancel the request, or abandon the work.

   The working area and the Preview window are cleared.

### *Keyboard Shortcut*

Alt-F-N

### *To open an existing file*

1. With any tool, open the File menu.

2. Select Open.

3. Double-click on the name of the CorelDraw file you want to open.

   You may have to change directories if the file is not in the current directory.

### *Keyboard Shortcut*

Ctrl-O

### *Note*

You can configure your WIN.INI file, use a batch file, or the DOS command line to load CorelDraw as Windows is loaded. See the Windows User Guide for more information.

# Stretch, Scale, and Mirror Objects

### Purpose

Changes the size, height, and width of objects. You also can use these commands to turn an object inside out. It is easy to create effects such as drop shadows and mirror images when these options are combined with other commands, such as Leave Duplicate.

### To stretch and scale with the mouse

1. Select the Pick tool from the Toolbox.

2. Click on the object so that the black square handles appear.

3. Place the cursor (which resembles a thin cross) on one of the handles and drag in the desired direction.

   Dragging a corner handle scales the object, but dragging any other handle stretches or squeezes the object.

4. Release the button when the dotted guide lines are the size or shape you want.

### To create a mirror image with the mouse

1. Select the Pick tool from the Toolbox.

2. Click on the object so that the black square handles appear.

3. Drag the mouse directly across the object in the desired direction.

4. Release the button when the dotted lines are in the size or shape you want.

   To obtain a perfect duplicate of the object and leave the original intact, you must drag the mouse, press the +key, and hold the **Constrain** key during the rest of the movement. Release the Constrain key after you release the mouse button.

### *To stretch, scale, and mirror using the Transform menu*

1. Select the Pick tool from the Toolbox.

2. Click on the object so that the black square handles appear.

3. From the Transform menu, select Stretch and Mirror.

4. Set the amount of Horizontal and Vertical Stretch in the appropriate entry boxes by either entering the numbers or clicking the arrows to the right of each box.

   or

   Click on the Horizontal and Vertical Mirror command buttons to set the values to -100 percent.

5. Click on the Leave Duplicate checkbox to leave a copy of the object in its existing location.

### *Notes*

The Status Line shows the exact amount of change for the current transformation to help size the object.

Pressing and holding the Constrain key limits size changes to 100 percent increments.

By clicking once on the selected object, you toggle between the Stretch and Scale and the Rotate and Skew modes.

To return the object to its original condition, see *Clear Transformations*.

# Technical Support

### *Purpose*

Enables you to get answers to operational problems you have with CorelDraw, or to get assistance with specific hardware configurational problems.

## To contact Technical Support

1. Make note of the exact problem that you are experiencing, what you were doing when it happened, and any error messages received.

2. Have the following information available:

   • The type of computer, video card, monitor, mouse, and printer you use.

   • The version numbers of DOS, Windows, and CorelDraw you run. (See the About entry in this book.)

   • The information in your CONFIG.SYS and AUTOEXEC.BAT files and the names of any other programs that were running when the problem occurred.

3. Call the CorelDraw Hotline at (613) 728-1990 between 8:30 a.m. to 7 p.m. Monday through Thursday, and from 8:30 a.m. to 5 p.m. on Fridays (Eastern Standard Time).

4. You also can FAX your questions to (613) 761-9175. This number differs from the FAX number listed in CorelDraw references printed before September 1990.

## Note

Corel provides a high-quality technical support team. Over the past few years the staff on the Corel Hotline has grown from one person to 19. All staff members are trained and very helpful.

# Undo/Redo

## Purpose

Enables you to restore the drawing to the state it was in before the last command was issued. This command is handy when a result is undesirable. If you are trying to choose between two options, just toggle between Undo and Redo.

### To restore a drawing

1. Open the Edit menu with any tool.

2. Select Undo.

You can follow the procedure and select Redo the second time.

### Keyboard Shortcut

Alt-Backspace for Undo only, Alt-E for Redo.

### Notes

You cannot use Undo/Redo on file operations such as Save or Open in connection with object selection methods such as Shift-Click or Marquee Select, or with the Zoom tool.

After you use another command, you cannot undo the previously issued command.

# Zoom

### Purpose

Enables you to define the area of the picture you want to see.

### To change the area displayed

1. Use any tool to select the Zoom tool.

2. Select one of the following icons:

- Use the + **Magnifying Glass** icon (Zoom In) to drag over any area in the Preview window. After you release the mouse button, the selected area fills the editing area.

- Use the –**Magnifying Glass** icon (Zoom Out) to revert the Preview to a view equal to the previous view or to double the area to twice that at the time.

- Use the 1:1 icon to change the view to approximately the actual size. The exact ratio varies depending on the type of monitor and the Windows Screen Driver in use.

- Use the All icon to place every object in the drawing (on or off the page) inside the Preview Window.

- Use the shadowed rectangle icon (Show Page) to shift view in the editing window to include the entire print area.

***Note***

The Zoom feature gives you control over the viewing area and, therefore, enhances objects you draw and increases the usefulness of other CorelDraw tools.

# CORELTRACE COMMAND REFERENCE

## About CorelTrace

CorelTrace is much more sophisticated than the Auto-trace command that is available in CorelDraw. With CorelTrace, you can convert PCX and TIF bitmap images into the Encapsulated Postscript (EPS) format. You then can edit these images in CorelDraw, export the images to another format, or use the images directly in programs such as Aldus PageMaker or Xerox Ventura Publisher. The original file is not changed, but a second file in vector format is made.

CorelTrace enables you to design an image in a paint program by scanning existing art or using bitmap clip art and converting it to a form you can edit with CorelDraw.

Converting existing images from bitmap into vector format offers these advantages:

- Vector images are resolution independent. Because bitmap images are really just a collection of dots, changing the size usually results in jagged edges when you print diagonal lines or curves. Vector files are created by using mathematical formulas to describe the shape of objects.

- A vector drawing may use only a fraction of the disk space that a bitmap image does. An uncompressed black and white bitmap image the size of a standard page, without grayscale or color information, requires more than a megabyte of disk space. Adding tone or color dramatically increases the amount of disk space needed.

CorelTrace does not interpret color or grayscale information when it creates a conversion file, and dither patterns used to emulate halftones in some files may produce unacceptable results. The program does a good job on plain PCX and TIF files.

# CorelTrace Interface

CorelTrace has a simple interface that uses only a few menus. The actual creation of a new file is handled by the computer. You simply load the program, tell the program which tracing method to use, which file to convert, and start the program. As the program converts the file, you can watch the tracing in a window. After all the files are traced, the window disappears and you can import the new files to CorelDraw or another program that can make use of the EPS format. (For more information on file format types, see *Import* and *Export*.)

CorelTrace contains two preset tracing modes: Normal Centerline and Normal Outline. Full Centerline tracing draws a line that follows the centerline of the lines it finds in the bitmap file. All line widths are controlled. This option is best suited for tracing images such as technical drawings and schematics.

The Outline method creates lines, curves, closed objects; fills closed paths; and works to determine the objects that make up the image. Segments vary in thickness.

The Centerline method is primarily designed for tracing lines, but it produces an outline if it detects a filled object in the bitmap image. It probably is best to use the Outline method when tracing bitmaps that contain mostly filled objects. Remember that Centerline is designed to follow the middle of a line and give a fixed line width to all lines. If most of the lines in a drawing are larger than six points, you should use the Outline method for tracing.

By using the Edit Options feature of CorelTrace, you can customize a combination of both the Centerline and Outline modes, as well as control such things as the thickness of lines drawn, and set how closely the trace will follow curves and lines. You even can create a copy that reverses black and white, yielding a negative image.

An extensive help system is available that contains basically all the information in the CorelTrace manual, and you can modify or add entries if you want.

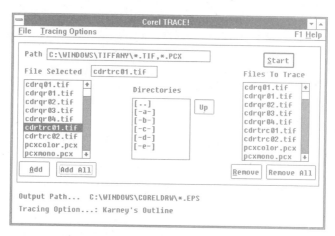

# Choosing Tracing Options

### Purpose

Enables you to select the best set of options for converting a given bitmap. Options include the default configurations, a predefined user configuration, or a new custom tracing configuration.

## To choose tracing options

1. With the mouse, select the Tracing Options menu.

   The menu opens and displays a list of the default and predefined user tracing configurations.

2. Select the tracing method you want to use.

   The name of the selected method appears on the last line of the CorelTrace Window and is marked with a checkmark in the menu list.

3. If you want to modify any of the settings for this tracing run, reopen the Tracing Options menu and select Edit Options.

4. Make any changes you want. (See *Custom Tracing Options* for more information.)

5. Click OK to confirm, or Cancel to abandon your changes.

# Custom Tracing Options

### Purpose

Enables you to create or modify a set of options for a tracing run and to save a collection of settings for future use. You can adjust CorelTrace to suit the needs of a particular job. The proof of a custom setting is in how well it does the job at hand. If you find that you have to a lot of cleanup on a specific file after you import it to CorelDraw, you may want to adjust the settings and retrace the image.

### To set custom tracing options

1. From the Main menu, select Tracing Options.

2. If required, click on the name of the current option set you want to revise if it already exists and repeat Step 1.

3. Select Edit Options.

   The Tracing Options dialog box contains eight major sections, most of which are controlled with radio buttons. The name of the function is listed for each section. Do the following steps as required:

4. Select either Outline Only or Centerline, and set the Maximum or Uniform Line Width for Centerline if desired.

   • Maximum Line Width is available only for the Centerline method. This option specifies the maximum thickness of the lines that will be created in the new file and is measured in pixels. Setting a lower value results in thinner and rougher lines.

   • Uniform Line is also an option used with Centerline tracing. This option forces all lines in the traced file to a specific width. Note that this option produces undesired results if the original drawing contains a number of different sized lines.

   • If Uniform Line is selected, set the width in pixels in the Width in Dots box.

5. Set the Curve Length by choosing one of the radio buttons.

   The shorter this option is set, the closer the tracing follows curves, producing more nodes per segment. Longer curves produce a smoother appearance.

6. Set the value for Convert Long Lines by choosing one of the radio buttons.

   Setting this option toward the curve end of the scale causes the program to create most of the segments in the new file as curves. Setting the option in the opposite direction produces more straight lines. Drawings such as schematics and forms may look better with more lines set in this option.

7. Set the **Fit Curve** value by choosing one of the radio buttons.

   The tighter the fit to curves, the closer the trace matches the original, and the larger the resulting file. If you have a very large object, a small setting may make it easier to import the object to CorelDraw.

8. Set the Sample Rate by choosing one of the three radio buttons.

   A coarse setting produces fewer nodes in the traced file, but a fine setting results in a greater number of nodes in a given object.

9. Set the amount of Edge Filtering by choosing one of three available radio buttons.

   Use this option if your original bitmap has jagged lines from resizing or low resolution.

10. Enter the setting for Maximum cluster size in the Remove Noise box.

    This setting is the smallest number of pixels in a cluster that will be placed in the trace file. Any smaller number will be considered background noise and not converted.

11. Type a name for the new set of options. The name can be 19 characters long and contain spaces. If there is already a name listed in the Option Name entry box, your new name overwrites the old version.

12. Is desired, choose Invert Bitmap.

13. Click OK to confirm your choices and return to the Main CorelTrace menu or Cancel to abandon the operation.

## Tip

Choose context-sensitive names for custom settings. For example, you may have one custom setting called Building Plans.

Be careful when you save custom settings. Note the name before you save your work. The name becomes the name for that collection. If the name exists, the old options are overwritten.

## Notes

Some simple planning before changing settings may help you get a better trace. Examine the image. Is it made up of lines, or does it have a lot of filled areas? Do you plan to use CorelDraw to clean up the image, or will it go straight into a desktop publishing program? What is the visual effect you are trying to achieve, and what is the quality of the original image? If you are experimenting with a grayscale TIF file to get a poster effect, the setting will be different than the settings for tracing a set of house plans.

Another good reason to plan is to reduce the file size when you trace complex images like celtic illuminated art or topographical maps. The tighter the match is to the original—the more nodes and larger the file. You may run out of memory or find that the result does not print or even fit into CorelDraw.

# Help

## Purpose

Provides information on program operations.

## To open and use the Help menu

1. With no other dialog boxes or menus open, click on the word Help, which appears in the upper right of the screen.

The Help information screen opens.

2. Click on the item you want to see from the table of contents.

3. Click on the scroll bars or the options at the top of the Help box to navigate as desired.

4. Click on Quit to exit.

### Keyboard Shortcuts

Press F1 to open and Alt-Q to quit Help.

### Note

You can customize help listings for CorelTrace. For more information enter the File Manager (Windows 3) or the DOS Executive. Double-click on the CORELHLP.EXE and read the listings for modifying help. You can incorporate small bitmap images into your help screens.

# Importing and Exporting CorelTrace Files to CorelDraw

### Purpose

Enables you to revise CorelTrace files, add EPS Headers, and export to formats supported by other programs.

### To import, edit, and export CorelTrace files

1. Finish conversion in CorelTrace. (See entry under *Tracing* in this section of the book.)

2. Close CorelTrace.

3. Open CorelDraw and select Import from the File menu.

4. Select the CorelTrace EPS format option.

5. Double-click on the name of the desired file in the File Section box.

The drawing is imported to CorelDraw as a group of objects. The Status Line indicates how many elements exist. You may want to enable the Preview window and use the Zoom tool to enlarge the drawing. Note that complex files may take considerable time to redraw on the screen.

6. Edit as usual in CorelDraw. Remember that you must Ungroup the tracing into separate objects to edit nodes and segments with the Shape tool.

7. After you complete work, save the drawing as a CorelDraw CDR file using the Save or Save As command.

8. You may use the Export option to save a version of the newly edited illustration. For more information see *Export*.

### Tip

Even though the CorelTrace file is already in EPS format, it does not include a header file. The header permits programs, such as Xerox Ventura Publisher, to display a bitmap image of the EPS file. Without this option, you cannot see how the file looks until it is printed.

### Note

Very complex drawings may not import or print. You can adjust settings in the CorelTrace Tracing Options to reduce the number of nodes created when the file is converted.

# Installation and System Requirements

### Purpose

Insures that CorelTrace runs smoothly on your system. Any computer that successfully runs CorelDraw 1.2 can operate CorelTrace, but there are some additional factors of which to be aware.

### *To run CorelTrace on a basic system you need the following:*

- An 80286, 80386, or 80486 computer that is compatible with Microsoft Windows 286 Version 2.03 or later.

- An EGA, Hercules, or VGA display card and monitor.

- A mouse or tablet with Windows support.

- A 640K of RAM memory and at least 2 megabytes of disk space available for handling Temp files.

As CorelTrace works, it writes information to a temporary file. Corel recommends that you have at least two megabytes of space, and four might be better for most users. A rough guide is to have available about ten times the amount of space the original file requires.

### *To set up a CorelTrace temporary file*

1. Make a backup copy of your AUTOEXEC.BAT file under the name AUTOEXEC.OLD by typing **RENAME AUTOEXEC.BAT AUTOEXEC.OLD** at the DOS prompt.

2. Load an editor or word processor that can generate an ASCII (plain text file).

3. Add the line **SET TEMP=C:\** or replace the C:\ with the name and path for the directory you want the files written to. Do not use the directory with your Windows program files.

4. Save the file as an ASCII text file.

5. You must reboot your computer for the change to take effect.

### *Note*

The actual size for the temp file for a given conversion is figured using the formula: image resolution (in dots per inch) squared times the image area (in square inches) divided by 2. For a full eight-by-ten inch page at 300 dpi, for example, the formula reads as follows:

300 x 300 x 80/2 = 3.6 megabytes

If you are planning to convert a full page bitmap, you need about four megabytes of free hard disk space for your TEMP file.

---
*Tip*

Close all other Windows and non-Windows applications when you convert files, especially more complicated bitmaps.

---
*Note*

If you do not have Version 1.2 of CorelDraw or later, you did not receive CorelTrace. Contact Corel Systems at (613) 728-8200 for upgrade information.

# Opening/Closing CorelTrace

---
*Purpose*

Brings up the program interface to begin using the application and to exit the program.

---
*To open CorelTrace*

1. Load Microsoft Windows if it is not active by typing **WIN** at the DOS prompt.

2. Double-click on the CorelTrace icon if using the Program Manager (it looks like a pencil tracing on two pieces of paper over a light bulb) or on the **CORELTRC.EXE** file name if you are using the File Manager.

---
*To close CorelTrace*

1. Close any open dialog boxes by clicking **OK** or **Cancel** to abandon the operation.

2. Click to open the File menu.

3. Click on the Exit option.

You are returned to the primary Windows level.

# Output Options

## *Purpose*

Although there is only one file output format from CorelTrace, you can select the directory in which to place your new files, as well as decide whether you want to be prompted when a name conflict is about to occur.

## *To set Output options*

1. Open the File menu in CorelTrace.

2. Select Output Options.

   The Output Options dialog box appears.

3. Choose Always replace, or Always prompt.

   If you choose Always replace, CorelTrace overwrites the file when a file by that name is already present in the chosen directory.

   If you choose Always prompt, a dialog box appears when a file with the same name is present in the active directory. If that occurs, follow these steps:

4. The Confirm dialog box appears.

5. Click on Yes to overwrite the file (the old version of the file will be destroyed) or NO to rename the new file.

   If you select No, the Output File section box appears, and the name of the conflicting file is shown in the Path box.

6. Enter a new name and path for the file you want to create.

7. Click OK to confirm or Cancel to abandon the operation.

# Preparing Bitmaps for Tracing

### Purpose

Obtains a bitmap image that you can trace, and provides an acceptable vector drawing for editing or printing. Proper preparation can reduce conversion and editing time, as well as memory and storage requirements.

### To prepare bitmaps for tracing

1. Work with TIF formats, if possible, to reduce file size.

2. Scan all images for conversion in the same run at the same resolution.

   Use the highest possible resolution, unless file size is a problem.

   Make sure that images are placed properly in the scanner to reduce jaggies.

   Inspect the scanned file and rescan if the contrast is low, the image is broken up, or many jaggies appear.

   Enlarge the original artwork if it is less than four-by-five inches in size to between four-by-five inches and five-by-seven inches.

   Use quality paper (such as Hammermill Laserprint), if you are printing a file to be scanned.

   Chartpak Workable Matte Fixative (available at art supply stores) darkens large areas of black in a laser printout.

   For grayscale art (such as photographs) increase contrast when scanning and lower the scanner resolution to reduce file size.

3. Clean up the bitmap image in a paint program if there are unwanted portions or a lot of "dirt" in the file.

   Crop any unwanted parts of the image.

Erase any text in the bitmap that can be redone inside or is to be edited in CorelDraw.

Remove any dots or small lines that were created by dust or dirt on the page or scanner.

4. Group similar images to be traced at the same time. Trace very complex or difficult images one at a time and observe the quality of the trace.

5. If a traced file looks as if it may be difficult to edit, consider improving the bitmap file or changing the CorelTrace option settings.

### Notes

No hard and fast rules apply for raster to vector conversion. Experience is the best way to develop an eye for choosing settings on your scanner and in CorelTrace.

Most black and white images of a reasonable size and complexity trace with one of CorelTrace's default option combinations.

# Tracing

### Purpose

Creates a vector-based copy of an existing bitmap image that you import to CorelDraw or another program that can make use of an Encapsulated Postscript File (EPS).

### To use Trace

1. Have Microsoft Windows running and close any unnecessary applications.

2. Load CorelTrace.

   The Main menu and dialog box appear.

3. Note that the output path shown in the lower left of the menu is as desired, and change it if required.

4. Note that the Tracing option shown in the lower left of the menu is correct. Change or modify it if required.

5. Use the selection box in the center of the dialog box to select the proper drive and directory.

   The available files based on the section filter in the upper left of the dialog box are shown in the Files Selected list on the left.

6. Click on the **Add All** command button to choose all of the file at once, double-click on a single file, or click on individual files and then click on the **Add** command button.

   The names of the selected files now appear in the Files To Trace box on the right of the screen.

7. Remove any unwanted files from the Files To Trace box by clicking on an individual file and then clicking the **Remove** command button, or click on the **Remove All** command button.

   If **Allways Prompt** is active, the Output Options dialog box prompts you to change the name in case of any file conflicts.

   The active Tracing window opens and shows the progress of each file as it is traced. The original bitmap shows as a gray and white image, and the trace is superimposed over it in black. Depending on the display card and monitor, the actual tracing may be of higher quality than the screen display.

8. When the files are finished, they are available in the chosen directory. Load them into CorelDraw or another program for editing and printing.

*Note*

   For more information on EPS files see the *Import* and *Export* listing in the Command Reference section.

# Index